U.S. MARIN
OPERATIONS A

MW01379590

COUNTDOWN
TO 13 DAYS
AND BEYOND

VMCJ-2

*To
Rau

[signature] Semper Fi
[signature] Wayne Whitten*

President Kennedy presenting NUC to VFP-62 withVMCJ-2 augmentation pilots at Key West November 26, 1962

NAVY UNIT COMMENDATION RIBBON

VMCJ-2 RECEIVED THE NUC FOR PHOTO AND ELECTRONIC RECONNAISSANCE OPERATIONS AGAINST CUBA FROM SEPTEMBER 1, 1960 - DECEMBER 1, 1962

COUNTDOWN TO 13 DAYS AND BEYOND

MARINE COMPOSITE RECONNAISSANCE SQUADRON -2

Colonel H. Wayne Whitten
USMC (ret)

COUNTDOWN TO 13 DAYS AND BEYOND
–U.S. MARINE AERIAL RECONNAISSANCE OPERATIONS
AGAINST CASTRO'S CUBA 1960-1990
© Copyright pending 2012. by H. Wayne Whitten, Colonel USMC
(Ret.) All rights reserved.

Second Edition (September 2012)
Published by: Colonel H. Wayne Whitten and Associates

ISBN: 978-0-87121-035-7

Cover photos are of a Chance Vought RF-8A Photo Crusader and Douglas EF-10B Skyknight from Marine Composite Reconnaissance Squadron 2 with flop-eared bunny logo from early 1960s. In later years the trademarked Playboy bunny was used with permission.

Cover Design, Book Design and Layout by:
Eli Blyden | www.CrunchTimeGraphics.NET

Printed in the United States of America by:
A&A Printing | www.PrintShopCentral.com

Contents

Foreword

Countdown To 13 Days And Beyond is a gripping memorialization of one of the most critical times in our nation's history, the Cuban Missile Crisis, and the part that Marine Corps aerial reconnaissance played in the discovery and tracking of the nuclear threat that came to be just 90 miles from our shores. The timing of this book is most appropriate as we near the 50th anniversary of those anxious days of October 1962 that threatened to turn the Cold War hot.

The focus of the book is on the role played by Marine Composite Reconnaissance Squadron 2 (VMCJ-2), which was based at MCAS Cherry Pt. North Carolina, but the author vividly details that story in context with then on-going events and the political decisions that shaped them. To that end, he recounts Castro's rise to power, the Bay of Pigs fiasco, and his build-up in military capability courtesy of the Soviet Union.

The author draws upon his previous treatise, *Silent Heroes*, to describe VMCJ-2's transition to the F3D-2Q (EF-10B) Skyknight electronic warfare aircraft, and how returning veterans from a deployment to the Pacific influenced the decision to begin "unofficial" electronic reconnaissance missions around Castro's Cuba. He then details the superb photographic reconnaissance capabilities of the squadron's new F8U-1P (RF-8A) Crusaders, setting the stage for employment of both aircraft to monitor evolving military activities in Cuba two years before the crisis began.

The book provides background on the advances in technology during the 1950s that includes ground based air defense radar and surface to air missile capabilities by our Cold War adversary, the USSR. This assists the reader in understanding why the build-up of these front line Soviet "defensive" capabilities in Cuba monitored by the Marines ultimately proved to be tell-tale signs of the secret installation of offensive ballistic missiles capable of hitting targets across the United States.

The confirmation of medium and intermediate range ballistic missile sites under construction by a U-2 spy plane on October 14 marked the commencement of the 13 day crisis that shook the world. The author picks up the story with the decision by President Kennedy to announce a blockade of Cuba and ordering low level photographic reconnaissance to get detailed pictures of the missile sites. He relates how and why VMCJ-2 was tasked to augment VFP-62, the Navy's counterpart squadron, with aircraft and aircrews for this critical operation. He writes about these low level missions flown by the Navy/Marine Corps team and provides some of the actual photographs used to convince JFK and our allies to stand eye to eye with Nikita Khrushchev and his surrogate, Fidel Castro.

We all know the result, Khrushchev blinked and the Marine and Navy reconnaissance squadrons were later presented the first ever Navy Unit Commendations (NUC) to be awarded in peacetime. In addition, all of the RF-8A pilots were awarded Distinguished Flying Crosses in recognition of the value of the intelligence they brought back from their missions over Cuba. Not content with concluding his book with the peaking of the crisis in Cuba and the political compromise that resulted, Colonel Whitten continues with a chapter devoted to electronic reconnaissance missions in the years that followed. The epilogue describes the author's personal experience from one of those missions.

General Jack Dailey, former Assistant Commandant of the Marine Corps, wrote in the foreword to the author's first book, *Silent Heroes*, that this was a book that needed to be written. His second book, *Countdown to 13 Days and Beyond*, is a book that needs to be read. It needs to be read by aviation historical buffs and by anyone who is interested in knowing the details of how intelligence was obtained that enabled President Kennedy to avert a nuclear confrontation with the Soviet Union.

–William A. "Art" Bloomer
Brigadier General, United States Marine Corps (Ret)

I owe a special thanks to Brigadier General Bloomer for his detailed review of *Countdown to 13 Days*, and his gracious foreword. Readers should note that he is one of the Marine Corps' most experienced reconnaissance and electronic warfare pilots, having flown the RF-8A, RF-4B, EF-10B, EA-6A and the EA-6B. He served in VMCJ-3 at MCAS El Toro and completed three tours with VMCJ-1 in the Pacific, flying over 300 reconnaissance and electronic combat missions in Vietnam. General Bloomer was just completing his first tour with VMCJ-1 in Japan in 1962 when the Cuban Missile Crisis began. He had his orders changed to immediately report back to VMCJ-3 as a contingency backup pilot for VMCJ-2 which was then deployed to Key West. Then Lieutenant Colonel Bloomer was the last commanding officer of VMCJ-1, retiring that distinguished unit's colors in September 1975.

Since his retirement he has been a mainstay in the Marine Corps Aviation Reconnaissance Association, serving twice as president.

–HWW

Preface

VMCJ-2 was awarded a Navy Unit Commendation (NUC) for the period September 1, 1960 through December 1, 1962 for aerial reconnaissance operations against Cuba that was of critical importance to our national interest. It was the first ever awarded to a Marine unit in peacetime. The following account of the squadron's historic efforts involving the F8U-1P/RF-8A photo and the F3D-2Q/ EF-10B EW aircraft is based largely on recollections of some of the decorated aircrews that flew the missions and from a variety of historical sources that made the Cuban Missile Crisis and its 13 days in October 1962 one of the most written about periods in our nation's history. It is intended as a tribute to all who served in the squadron during this perilous period which brought us to the brink of a disastrous nuclear war.

My inspiration for this humble attempt to relate the VMCJ-2 story came from the latest and most revealing of the published sources, <u>One Minute to Midnight</u> by Michael Dobbs. It also has a personal significance to me as at the time I was a senior at the University of Florida in Gainesville, and a corporal in the USMCR awaiting graduation in six months and commissioning as a 2nd lieutenant. I remember well seeing the convoys of troops and equipment moving through town headed for South Florida ports to support a Cuba invasion that seemed sure to come. Meanwhile my wife (eight months pregnant with our first son), and I like everyone else stayed glued to the radio or TV for news.

Ironically, years later I too joined VMCJ-2 and was involved in a confrontation with Castro's air force which is included as an epilogue.

–HWW

VMCJ-2 Receives Navy Unit Commendation

By Sgt. Bob Ambrose

At ceremonies here Monday, VMCJ-2 became the first Marine Corps unit to receive the Navy Unit Commendation (NUC) medal during peace time.

A streamer, representing the NUC award, was attached to the photo squadron's colors by BrigGen. Paul J. Fontana, 2d Wing Commanding General, during Monday's formal ceremonies. BrigGen. George S. Bowman Jr., new Assistant 2d Wing Commander, witnessed the ceremony.

The citation, awarded by the Secretary of the Navy, reads in part: "For exceptionally meritorious service during the period Sept. 1, 1960 to Dec 1, 1962, in connection with the planning and executing of aerial reconnaissance missions in support of operations of the utmost importance to the security of the United States.

"The consistent and outstandingly high record of accomplishment attained by VMCJ-2 attests to the professional competence, diligence, and resourcefulness of its officers and men."

VMCJ-2's mission is to conduct day and night aerial photographic reconnaissance, airborne electronic and communications counter measure operations.

Aircraft used in the squadron include the EF-10B "Skynight," which is used for electronic reconnaissance and counter measure missions, and the RF-8A "Crusader," specially configured for aerial photographic reconnaissance operations.

VMCJ-2 is presently commanded by LtCol. George H. Dodenhoff.

QUADRON CITED—BrigGen. Paul J. Fontana, 2d Wing Commanding General, attaches a Navy Unit Commendation streamer to the colors of VMCJ-2 during formal ceremonies here Monday. (Photo by Sgt. Bill Harmon)

Acknowledgements

First, for this limited reader edition I chose not to include chapter end notes referencing specific sources. This is due in part to the fact that there is so much open source material in either published form or internet accessible files about Castro, the failed Bay of Pigs operation, and the Cuban Missile Crisis, that it is often difficult to make specific attributions. Secondly, those well documented events are mainly used as a backdrop, for the focus of this book is on the contributions of the Marines in VMCJ-2 to that history. I do want to cite upfront my main sources and strongly recommend the readers obtain their own copies of the published books, and look to the internet for the writings of so many others.

Without question I would never have undertaken this project if I had not read *One Minute to Midnight by* Michael Dobbs. (Alfred A. Knopf, New York 2008, ISBN 978-1-4000-4358-3). Dobbs' work is unique as he wrote it from both a journalist and historian's viewpoint and as such he found through his extensive research several significant inaccuracies in previous works to include some by senior government participants. He was able to exploit a lot of previously classified U.S. documents, thanks to the efforts of the independent National Security Archive which forced the release of the majority of the holdings by the State Department historian. But most importantly, Dobbs interviewed more than 100 veterans of the Cuban Missile Crisis from all of the countries involved including the Marine Corps pilots who flew the critical low level reconnaissance missions along with their Navy counterparts. His research at that late date uncovered one of the most shocking secrets of all , the previously unreported fact that the Russians had cruise missiles in place that were to be used to wipe out the huge U.S. base at Guantanamo Bay at the start of hostilities. His riveting day by day account of the 13 most perilous days in our nation's history is by and large the source of most of my writings for the associated chapters.

Secondly, I drew extensively on the State Department files that are available now on the internet as the *Foreign Relations of the United States series, 1961-1963, Volumes X,XI,XV (* Washington D.C. : U.S. Government Printing Office, 1997,1996,1994.) Similarly, I found a significant amount of relevant information about the various operational plans and activities from the senior combatant commands from internet files made available by the Naval Historical Center. The Central Intelligence Agency (CIA) has also released numerous previously highly classified documents which give a good account of the information available that may or may not have been acted on. A telling report by Colonel Jack Hawkins, USMC (ret), relating his side of the failed Bay of Pigs invasion by the Cuban exile brigade he helped train for the CIA is also available on the internet.

A significant part of this project relating to the development and operation of the F3D-2Q/EF-10B Skyknight aircraft, is drawn directly from my previous book *SILENT HEROES – U.S. Marines and Airborne Electronic Warfare 1950-2012*,(Banner Digital Printing and Publishing, Inc. Homewood, Alabama, 2011).

The significance of the Soviet-designed SA-2 surface-to-air missile system to the Cuban Missile Crisis warrants references to its early deployments and employments as well as its capabilities which are related in great detail in Steven J. Zaloga's book *Red SAM: The SA-2 Guideline Anti-Aircraft Missile,* (Osprey Publishing Ltd., New York, 2007).

Many of the anecdotal accounts of the actual deployments and operational missions flown by the Marines is documented in a book by Chief Warrant Officer-2 (Ret.) J.T. O'Brien, a participant himself. (*Top Secret, A Ready Room History of Electronic Warfare and Photo Reconnaissance in Marine Corps Aviation 1940-2000*, (Anaheim: Equidata 2004).

A new book about the role of Navy Light Photographic Squadron 62 in the Cuban Missile Crisis, which I along with some of the Marine pilots that flew with the squadron contributed to, was published in August 2012 by Osprey Publishing. It is *Blue Moon over Cuba: Aerial*

Reconnaissance during the Cuban Missile Crisis by Capt. William B. Ecker, USN (ret.) and Kenneth V. Jack. Kenneth Jack is the webmaster for the old photographic squadron, and the website www.vfp62.com is highly recommended as a reference.

Peter Mersky's **RF-8 Crusader Units Over Cuba And Vietnam,** (Osprey Publishing, Oxford, UK 1999), is a must read for photo reconnaissance enthusiasts as it details aircraft and camera systems with many photographs.

Lastly, but most importantly, I gratefully acknowledge the contributions of many of the Marine veterans that this book is about, as I relied heavily on their inputs, be they from written communications, or via personal or telephonic interviews dating back to 2008. Foremost in that group is the late Colonel Benjamin B. Skinner USMC (Ret.), an early participant in both electronic and photo reconnaissance of Castro's Cuba in 1960, and then a plank owner in the Commander-in-Chief- Atlantic (CINCLANT) Joint Reconnaissance Center (JRC) that oversaw all reconnaissance operations against Cuba from 1962 on. Colonel Skinner would later command VMCJ-2 in 1968.

The reader is also encouraged to visit the Marine Corps Aviation Reconnaissance Association's website at www.mcara.us for related material about the aircraft and units involved.

Except as noted, the pictures used in this book are from open sources to the best of my knowledge.

Prologue

When the Korean War ended in a stalemate and shaky truce in July 1953, the so-called Cold War resumed in earnest. The U.S. and the West were confronted by the communist menace led by the Soviet Union, which exerted its power and influence from Eastern Europe across the globe, often aided and abetted by its giant neighbor China. Both had demonstrated their willingness to extend military as well as political support to North Korea, a small bordering state seemingly off the world's center-stage. That conflict was restricted to the employment of conventional forces and weapons due to a conscious decision by the U.S. not to use tactical nuclear weapons for fear of the conflict evolving into another world war. This came at a time when the U.S. held a clear numerical advantage in nuclear weapons and aircraft delivery means over their Soviet adversaries. That gap in nuclear capability would be narrowed significantly during the decade of the fifties when long range ballistic missiles began to replace manned aircraft as delivery platforms.

As we began the 1960s, fear of a nuclear war had become part of our national psyche. Bomb shelters were constructed and stocked by private individuals, and all across America buildings carried signs pointing toward public fall-out shelters. School children were taught how to "duck and cover" under their desks, and routine drills were conducted by their teachers. In retrospect, this was seen as giving the populace a measure of relief, at least in their minds, but those in the know realized it would likely be all for naught in the event of a massive nuclear attack.

The concept of Mutually Assured Destruction (MAD) was adopted as a defense strategy and many thought its acronym actually served us best as leaders on both sides had to take note. Soon after the start of the new decade the Cold War would take a chilling turn of events that threatened to turn it red hot.

USAF Strategic Air Command (SAC) B-52 Stratofortress, America's frontline nuclear bomber for over 35 years.

CHAPTER ONE

Decade of the 50s – Advances in Aircraft, Radars and Missiles

Although the most significant advancements in military capability on both sides during the 1950s was in the strategic sector which commanded the lion share of the budget, technological changes influenced the tactical air forces as well. Tactical jet aircraft had come into their own during the Korean War and afterwards there was a wave of new developments leading to the U.S Air Force fielding of its Century series fighter/ attack aircraft, beginning with the F-100 Super Sabre. The Navy did likewise with a rather quick introduction of higher performance aircraft to replace their Korean War vintage F9F Panthers and F2H Banshee jets, followed soon after by a series of more advanced naval fighters to include the F8U Crusader. The Marine Corps aircraft wings were similarly upgraded and by the late 1950s employed an all jet fighter/attack fleet.

Advancements in radar technology were also fast paced in the 50s, both for ground and airborne applications. Although the latest fighter aircraft still depended on ground control intercept radars for assignment of targets, many were equipped with fire control radars that allowed gun and later missile engagements at night and periods of reduced visibility. On the ground the Soviets heavily invested in military radar development and by the mid-50s had deployed a vast early warning and ground control intercept network covering their vital economic and defense infrastructure. This network not only supported employment of their fighter/interceptor force against the Western bomber threat but also fed a new generation of mobile radar controlled anti-aircraft artillery (AAA) weaponry to support tactical forces. Of necessity, they later turned their attention to development of sophisticated surface–to-air missile systems and their associated radars. This was driven by the realities of nuclear war where a single long-range bomber could deliver a crippling blow, and fighter aircraft could not be counted on to preclude one or two from slipping through.

In late 1953, the Soviets initiated design and development of the S-75 SAM system with the intent to deploy it to support cities and bases throughout the country. It would later become the most widely deployed and employed SAM system in the world, known more by its Western names the SA-2. The S-75 was designed around a new V-750 (Guideline) missile that initially had a maximum altitude of about 70,000 feet which was above the operating altitudes of conventional bombers. It was well into flight testing by July 4, 1956 when they were surprised by the first overflight of an American U-2 spy plane flying at altitudes well above 70,000 feet. After a second U-2 overflew Moscow the next day, Chairman Nikita Khrushchev was infuriated and ordered a modification to the missile design to boost its maximum altitude to 80,000 feet.

The S-75 entered service in 1957 and was first deployed around key cities and defense facilities especially those associated with development and testing of strategic ballistic missiles. President Eisenhower was concerned that a U-2 would be eventually be downed by the new SAM and restricted U-2 overflights of the USSR heartland from late 1957 through 1959. His concerns were somewhat validated by the downing of a Taiwanese RB-57D at 65,500 feet on October 7, 1959 by a Russian-manned S-75 site protecting a nuclear test facility in neighboring China. In 1960, the demands for strategic intelligence forced Eisenhower into taking the risk, and the CIA's U-2 overflights of key test sites in the USSR were resumed. On May Day 1960 his fears were realized when a U-2 was shot down by an S-75 and the pilot, Francis Gary Powers, was captured. With that the U-2 was banned from overflight of the USSR but was still employed in China, the Mideast and Korea. The new spy satellites would begin to pick up coverage of strategic targets in 1960, including GRAB the first electronic intelligence (ELINT) satellite.

On the tactical warfare front, the rapidly evolving threat created a near insatiable demand for all forms of intelligence to support aircraft mission planning. In this pre-satellite era tactical aerial reconnaissance was a major military function performed by dedicated aircraft of all of the U.S. services. In addition to a new generation of jet photo aircraft, electronic reconnaissance variants of the Navy's A3D Skywarrior and the USAF B-66 Destroyer began supporting collection of Signals Intelligence (SIGINT) and/or ELINT data.. In the late 1950s the U.S. Marine Corps joined their larger service counterparts in this migration to an all jet reconnaissance force.

Russian Guideline SAM on its launcher

CHAPTER TWO

VMCJs Transition to F3D-2Qs and F8U-1Ps

The Marines had transitioned their photo reconnaissance squadrons (VMJs) to jets during the Korean War, but afterwards their three composite squadrons (VMCs), tasked to perform electronic reconnaissance, remained equipped with the propeller-driven AD-5Ns , the latest in the highly successful Douglas Skyraider series. That would dramatically change in the late 1950s, about the same time as their photo and composite squadrons would merge to form composite reconnaissance squadrons or VMCJs.

As the Marines joined the other services in moving to faster, single seat, fighter aircraft, farsighted Marines realized that these modern jets would need support from dedicated electronic warfare (EW) aircraft. For the most part tactical aircraft were not exposed to radar controlled AAA in Korea and VMC-1's first generation EW aircraft were exclusively tasked to perform electronic reconnaissance. Given the proliferation of threat radar controlled weapons systems after Korea it was clear that tactical aircraft would need electronic counter measures (ECM) or radar jamming support to carry out their close air support and interdiction missions. They also knew that effective support for these aircraft hinged to a large degree on an EW platform with comparable performance. The propeller-driven AD-5Ns were serving the Marine Corps EW community well at the time but training still was heavily oriented towards independent electronic reconnaissance missions that masked the performance gap with jet fighters.

Fortunately, the transition of the Navy and Marine Corps night fighter squadrons from the Douglas F3D-2 Skyknights to single seat aircraft freed up these twin engine, dual seat jets with lots of service life remaining. This aircraft was familiar to many of the VMC's enlisted Electronic Counter Measures Operators (ECMOs) who had flown it in Korea as airborne intercept operators. Like the AD-5 Skyraiders, the F3D-2 Skyknights had the same designer, Douglas Aircraft Company's famed Robert Heinemann, and there were a lot of similarities including the wide, dual place cockpit. The F3D-2 also was characterized by its large bulbous nose which housed the air intercept radar and contributed to the nickname "Willie the Whale". It was evident that it had a lot of easily accessible space for installation of a robust EW suite once the radar systems were removed. Although it was a straight wing, low performance jet that was not compatible with new carrier decks, it appeared to be a natural fit for Marine EW applications. One drawback with the F3D-2 was the lack of ejection seats. In an emergency the crew had to use an escape chute that extended from the cockpit to the belly of the aircraft to parachute out. This precluded bailing out at low altitudes and made escape in other than controlled situations difficult, a problem that would haunt Marine aircrews in later years.

Many officers and senior enlisted men in VMC-3 in 1955 had served with the first EW units in Korea that flew aircraft modified by Marines themselves. Those who saw the F3D-2 as the next generation EW platform also knew that the quickest way to gain HQMC support for a formal modification program was to develop a prototype themselves. Once again two of the Marine EW pioneers dating back to the TBM-3Q Avengers, Warrant Officer Joe Bouher and Master Sergeant "Doc" Grimes, stepped forward. They would play a lead role in the in-house conversion of the F3D-2s which was initiated by VMC-3 at MCAS El Toro in late spring of 1955. The first aircraft selected for modification was bureau number 124620 which had served with VMF(N)-513 in Korea. Later bureau number 125786 became the second prototype.

The prototype work moved swiftly during the summer of 1955 and the receiving system and related components carried over from the AD-5Ns were installed and tested by August. Sergeant John C. Cleveland, one of the Marine electronic technicians and ECMOs working on the prototypes, logged his first operational training flight in bureau number 125786 on August 26, 1955. This marked one of the earliest flights of a U.S. tactical EW jet aircraft although the reconnaissance version of the Douglas B-66 Destroyer was under production for the USAF Tactical Air Command during the latter half of 1955.

Captain Jim Janke USMC (Ret.) was an enlisted electronic technician working on the F3D-2Q prototypes in VMC-3 (later VMCJ-3) at MCAS El Toro, CA. in 1955-1956. He reenlisted as a corporal for ECMO training and deployed to Japan in 1958 with VMCJ-3. Janke recalls one of the goals of the conversion was to significantly improve the active ECM or jamming capability over the AD-5Ns. This meant the Marines had to find suitable systems and components from a variety of sources and develop an integration plan. The selected ECM package included two ALT-2 noise or continuous wave jammers that were installed internally with antennas located in the nose compartment. Wiring provisions were added to control additional jammers mounted in removable pods on the two wing stations or accommodate carriage of chaff pods. This ECM suite was incrementally installed and tested over several months after integration of the receiving system. Final technical and operational flight tests were performed at the White Sands Missile Range in New Mexico and at the Navy's China Lake California test ranges. The aircraft and its EW systems performed well during these tests and the first prototype was officially designated as an F3D-2Q in February 1956. Ironically, that same month the first USAF RB-66C electronic reconnaissance aircraft was delivered to Shaw AFB, South Carolina.

All of the wiring changes and structural modifications were documented for subsequent submission of a formal engineering change proposal to the Navy Bureau of Aeronautics. Eventually both Douglas Aircraft Company and the Navy aircraft Overhaul and Repair (O&R) facility at NAS North Island, California provided technical assistance for this endeavor. Headquarters Marine Corps subsequently sponsored a 35 aircraft retrofit program in FY-57 that was executed by O&R North Island. The first of the production F3D-2Qs were delivered to VMCJ-3 in December 1956. The squadron would complete the transition to the F3D-2Qs in 1957 and deploy with the Marine Corps first jet EW aircraft to MCAS Iwakuni, Japan in August, 1958.

VMCJ-2, based at MCAS Cherry Point, North Carolina, completed the transition to the F3D-2Qs in 1958, and the next year began its transition from the F9F-8P Photo Cougar to the new Chance-Vought F8U-1P photo Crusader. The F8U-1P photo reconnaissance version of the Crusader first flew on December 17, 1956 and entered service with the Navy in late 1957. It was slightly faster than the fighter version and had longer unrefueled range. An F8U-1P was selected by the Navy to set a transcontinental speed record under Project Bullet in July, 1957. Test pilot Major John H. Glenn, later one of the first astronauts, flew bureau number 144608 across the U.S. at a record average speed of 725.25 miles per hour.

The photo Crusader was designed to carry a variety of cameras enabling it to provide effective photo coverage from tree top level to 50,000 feet. The forward fuselage of the fighter was squared off to allow for three camera stations in the fuselage and a forward firing station under the air scoop. Fuselage station 2 normally housed trimetogen panoramic cameras to give horizon-to-horizon coverage, while Stations 3 and 4 held cameras in bays on either side that took either vertical or oblique photography. The forward station was used mostly for low level missions providing coverage along the flight path ahead. Film size was initially 70 MM or 2.5 inch square, but in later years five inch formats were introduced with improved image motion compensation.

VMCJ-1, based at MCAS El Toro, California, was the first of the Marine composite reconnaissance squadrons to transition to the F8U-1Ps and in October, 1959 was the first to deploy with the new aircraft to Japan. VMCJ-2 completed its transition to the photo Crusader in 1959. VMCJ-2's pilots, like their west coast counterparts, maintained their aircraft carrier qualifications.

VMCJ-2 served as the Second Marine Aircraft Wing's "Eyes and Ears". With the transition to new jet EW and photo reconnaissance aircraft complete in 1959, the squadron had the best tactical capabilities our nation had to offer. The timing could not have been better. Within a year the squadron would take on a new mission that would begin a countdown to a super-power confrontation that posed the greatest threat to the United States since WW II if not ever.

Chance Vought F8U-1P/RF-8A Photo Crusader
Pilot's viewfinder is shown with nose cone open. Station 1's forward firing camera window is under the air scoop, with side windows for stations 2 and 3 also visible.

VMCJ-3 F3D-2Q Skyknight over MCAS Iwakuni Japan 1958

VMCJ-3 exploited the F3D-2Q Skyknight's electronic reconnaissance capabilities in the western Pacific flying Shark Fin missions in 1958-1959.

Early ELINT Analysis Workbench

CHAPTER THREE

Castro's Rise and Reconnaissance Begins

In January 1959, Fulgencio Batista, the long term brutal dictator of Cuba, was finally overthrown by a rebel group led by Fidel Castro and his brother Raul after years of fighting dating back to July 26, 1953. The rebels had named their cause the 26th of July Movement honoring the date of the first overt act against Batista. Fidel Castro, at age 32, was sworn in as leader of the revolutionary government. At first disavowing he was a communist, Castro quickly moved to consolidate his power and seized all foreign assets in Cuba which were largely owned by Americans. It would be just the start of what was clearly an anti-American campaign as noted in Castro's near daily rhetoric. Upper and middle class Cubans, the most affected by Castro's edicts, soon began to leave the island in large numbers by any available means, and many of them settled in South Florida around Miami. They would become quite vocal in calling attention to the deteriorating human rights situation in Castro's Cuba, and influenced the policies of the U.S. government for generations.

By 1960, President Eisenhower had long recognized that Castro had no intention of establishing any form of open democracy in Cuba, and was quickly moving to solidify his government along typical communist lines. With the Cold War ongoing, this sent up a proverbial red flag, and on March 17, 1960 President Eisenhower moved to support a counter revolution by authorizing the Central Intelligence Agency (CIA) to initiate a covert action plan to overthrow the Castro regime. The initial plan included training of a Cuban exile brigade in Guatemala that would be covertly inserted and linked up with anti-Castro rebels who were already active in a remote mountain area. The hope and expectation was that this effort would result in an uprising by the Cuban people. The plan would undergo several changes in the following months. A key one was a decision to have the exile brigade (Brigade 2506) conduct an invasion after the strength of the rebels in the mountains was deemed too weak to lead the revolt.

With an amphibious landing now the focus of the plan for committing the exile brigade, the CIA had Marine Colonel Jack Hawkins assigned to lead the planning and training for what now was called Operation Zapata. Hawkins reported for duty on September 1, 1960 from his previous assignment as commander of amphibious forces at Little Creek, Virginia. He was a 1939 Naval Academy graduate who first served in China, then on to the Philippines at the start of World War II. Hawkins was captured at Corregidor and escaped from the Japanese after 11 months and joined a guerilla group for seven months before being rescued. He later participated in the

Okinawa campaign and was involved in planning of the Inchon amphibious landing early in the Korean War. He was an amphibious warfare instructor for three years prior to taking command at Little Creek.

Colonel Hawkins reported to Richard Bissell, the overall CIA lead for Operation Zapata. He ultimately was responsible for training a ragtag brigade of some 1500 Cubans with little or no formal military training to conduct a rather complex amphibious operation in just over six months. The original landing was to be at dawn over the beaches  near Trinidad on the southeast coast. The landing site was over 250 miles from Havana and adjacent to a mountain range that would afford the brigade cover for guerilla operations if they were unable to maintain a foothold long enough for other aspects of the plan to bring them relief. A river to the north and a swamp on the east provided added measures of security and would also channel Castro's responding forces into a kill zone. A key element of the plan was for a series of surprise air strikes to be carried out against Castro's airfields to gain air superiority and allow for continuous close air support during the critical landing phase.

Ironically the same month that Hawkins took the lead for the exile Cuban operation, VMCJ-2 began to fly electronic reconnaissance "training" missions around the island. Although not privy to any of the plans to overthrow Fidel Castro, the potential threat from a communist state just 90 miles off the shores of the United States was not lost on Marines from the Second Marine Aircraft Wing or VMCJ-2. During the past year several of the ECMOs who had made the first deployment to Japan with VMCJ-3 flying the F3D-2Q s returned home and joined VMCJ-2. At that point, all of them were either enlisted men or warrant officers promoted from the ranks, many with electronics or avionics backgrounds. During their 15 month tour in the Far East they had gained extensive experience with the modified Skyknights flying electronic reconnaissance missions around the periphery of North Korea, China and Russia under the Joint Chiefs of Staff (JCS) controlled Peacetime Aerial Reconnaissance Program (PARPRO).

On these missions code named Shark Fins, the F3D-2Q had proven to be an excellent platform for collection of ELINT data on numerous front-line Soviet designed military radars. The receiving system covered most of the operating frequencies of the Soviet radars and flying at altitudes around 30,000 feet many of the early warning and ground control intercept radars could be detected up to 200 miles away. With the benefit of an on-board direction finding capability, the location of the intercepted radars could be determined with reasonable accuracy during post flight analysis using the pilot's navigation logs if electronic navigation aids were available. The radar signals were also recorded on magnetic tape and on film of the ECMO's displays for post-flight analysis that confirmed the key operating parameters such as pulse width, scan rate, and pulse repetition frequency. The ECMOs had gained a solid reputation in the Pacific for the quality of their final product which was forwarded to the theater ELINT center for further processing and correlation with national electronic order of battle databases. Now they were to see that experience pay-off in their own backyard.

For some time, VMCJ-2 had been flying routine navigational missions with their Skyknights into NAS Leeward Point at the Guantanamo Naval Base in southeast Cuba from NAS Boca Chico at Key West. To the newly joining veterans of the Pacific operations it seemed like a natural evolution to exploit these training flights for ELINT collection against Castro's Cuba. Their ideas were put on paper and carried to the wing staff by the squadron commander who immediately saw the upside of conducting unofficial electronic reconnaissance missions under the guise of routine navigation training. The plan was approved and from September 1960 on the squadron would fly a series of monthly electronic reconnaissance missions around Castro's Cuba.

Then Sergeant Jim Janke, one of the veteran ECMOs from VMCJ-3, recalls being on a detachment of four F3D-2Qs for what was likely the second monthly deployment in late October 1960. According to his flight logs, he flew two missions out of Key West on October 28 and another on the 29th before flying into Guantanamo on the 30th,and returning to Key West on the 31st. Retired Colonel Ben Skinner, later a commanding officer of VMCJ-2, noted from his flight logs that he had entries for piloting F3D-2Q missions out of Key West from November 15-17, 1960. Colonel Skinner, then a captain, also provided the author a personal account of the first official Marine photo reconnaissance missions over Cuba.

Colonel Skinner recalled accompanying Major Dayton Robinson, the squadron operations officer, to a meeting shortly before Christmas of 1960 with the Second Marine Aircraft Wing's Assistant Chief of Staff Intelligence (G-2). At the meeting the VMCJ-2 officers received a classified briefing on priority requirements to obtain photo coverage of suspected military sites under construction on some small islands on the south coast of Cuba near the Isle of Pines. Other requested coverage was below Cienfuegos near Trinidad. Additionally, tasking was received to provide a mosaic map of the Guantanamo Bay naval base to assist in planning for defense of this large isolated U.S. facility actually located on the communist-run island.

On December 27, Captain Skinner led a section of F8U-1P photo Crusaders down to NAS Leeward Point at Guantanamo with Captain Jim Reed as his wingman. A supporting detachment of photographic and maintenance personnel followed via Marine transport aircraft. On December 28, the two pilots flew two sorties each from Guantanamo to cover the coastal targets some 200 miles to the north. They then flew sorties on the 29th and 30th to cover the Guantanamo confines before returning to MCAS Cherry Point on New Year's Eve.

Colonel Skinner recalls receiving confirmation that their first day's film was okay from his photo technicians, but it was sent back to Cherry Point for analysis and he never was briefed on what was found. By contrast, the Guantanamo film was processed and the mosaic map made available to the squadron later in accordance with normal procedures. The background on the requirements for coverage of the coastal areas has never been confirmed despite the exhaustive research and documentation of the events leading up to the invasion by the Cuban exile brigade in April, 1961. After discussions with Colonel Skinner while conducting research for this book, he agreed with the author that it was highly likely that Colonel Jack Hawkins was the source of the requirement. The designated landing site for the invasion at that time was the beaches near Trinidad. It follows that the planners were in need of updated photos of the approaches to the landing beaches, and of the adjacent areas where there might be military activity. It is logical that Colonel Hawkins used his Marine Corps connections to obtain the photo coverage using a cover story typical of CIA operations. In any event there is no plausible way the Second Marine Aircraft Wing G-2 could have tied the Crusader missions to the defense of Guantanamo some 200 miles away!

VMCJ-2 SENIOR ENLISTED ELECTRONIC COUNTERMEASURES OPERATORS (ECMOS) 1962
Back Row L-R Howard Meskin, Jerry O'Brien, Sam Gill, Bill Fleming, WO-1 Joe Stone, Front Row L-R Sam Figueroa, Fred Killebrew, Meek Kiker, Norm Charboneau and William Wood.

CHAPTER FOUR

Bay of Pigs Fiasco and
the Soviet Military Build-Up

As we entered the new year of 1961, the Cuban situation had continued to heat up and it soon became evident that the problem would be left to the incoming administration of President John F. Kennedy to deal with. No one expected it to later define his presidency. As President Eisenhower's parting shot he broke relations with Castro's government on January 3rd. The president-elect had been briefed on the CIA plan to overthrow Castro and the role of Brigade 2506 during the transition period. He knew it would be one of the first major foreign policy decisions he would have to make as the planned invasion was scheduled for April.

Meanwhile down at MCAS Cherry Point, the New Year brought a heightened awareness of the troubled island nation to the members of VMCJ-2. The short-notice deployment of the photo detachment to Guantanamo Bay at Christmas time was followed up with a second detachment according to Colonel Skinner. Captain H.C. Perkins led that deployment late in January which continued the mapping of the naval base environs and the fence line that separates the U.S. controlled area and communist Cuba. It is not known if other targets were covered as well. At some point later coverage of the Guantanamo fence line would become a recurring task for VMCJ-2's photo Crusaders and detachments would be sent out quarterly if not monthly for years to come. This meant the entire squadron was caught up in the Cuban "affair" as the monthly deployments of the F3D-2Qs to Key West continued throughout the year. Some would say this was the beginning of the VMCJ-2 mystique that would be added to in the years ahead and this before their famous Playboy bunny logo came on the scene!

Right after President Kennedy's inauguration, CIA officials met with senior members of the departments of State and Defense to review the plan for Operation Zapata. The President himself did not call a special meeting on the subject until mid-March which was after the date the CIA had wanted a decision to proceed. In the meantime there were discussions within the administration and the State Department's concerns that the U.S. could not afford to be implicated in the scheme to overthrow Castro's government became paramount, especially if there was no established threat to our security. At that point Castro had received a series of weapon shipments from communist bloc countries, but there was no evidence they included modern aircraft or rockets. It was noted that some Cuban pilots were receiving jet training in Czechoslovakia and that could eventually change the assessment.

Later, at the president's meeting he made it clear that he wanted plausible deniability of U.S. involvement in the exile operation. The planned daylight invasion in the Trinidad area was deemed too visible and characteristic of a U.S. amphibious operation. The CIA was directed to find an alternative landing site in a remote area and execute the operation under the cover of darkness. The other area of concern about deniability was the planned air strikes by the exiles against Castro's revolutionary air force that were to come from an airbase in Nicaragua. One of the cover stories was that the air strikes came from defecting Cuban air force pilots who were to land in Florida after raiding their former bases, with others diverting to an airfield controlled by the exiles for sustained support. This drove a requirement for an airfield in close proximity to the landing area to give credibility to the story that the sustaining air cover came from Cuban soil. Colonel Hawkins options were therefore limited and ultimately the infamous swampy Bay of Pigs area was selected as an alternate, although it had many obvious disadvantages. The site was much closer to Havana and Castro's opposing forces, lacked access roads and a viable port, and most importantly, was separated by a swamp from the safety of the Escambray mountains and rebel support. Further, the greater populated Trinidad area was thought to be more friendly to the rebel cause. Hawkins related later that he went to Bissell with his misgivings about the viability of the revised plan without U.S. military support, but the CIA lead chose not to pursue the matter in fear of the entire operation being called off. Historians are still split on whether the president was made aware of all the issues. Regardless, soon after hearing Soviet Chairman Nikita Khrushchev publicly describe the conflicts in Vietnam and Cuba as "wars of national liberation" that deserved USSR support, he authorized execution of Operation Zapata.

On April 15, eight B-26Bs flown by exile pilots from a secret base in Nicaragua attacked several Cuban air force bases but only managed to knock out about one half of Castro's few attack aircraft. Two of the exile pilots landed their planes in south Florida after suffering damage from ground fire. Despite warnings from his military leadership, the planned second strike to gain the needed air superiority was canceled by order of President Kennedy, who feared it would implicate the U.S. As planned, the landing by Brigade 2506 went down in the early morning hours of April 17, with a total of 1,453 men getting ashore from the invasion "fleet" of four landing and supply ships. The specifics of Operation Zapata were poorly kept secrets and Castro's forces were ready and able to respond. His remaining attack aircraft quickly retaliated by bombing and strafing the exposed exile forces and their ships. A key supply ship with most of the sustaining ammunition and supplies was sunk and the others forced to retreat. Castro himself led a decisive counter attack by his armor-equipped ground forces, and the exiles were doomed on day one. Although the fight went on for three days, in the end their losses were 115 dead and nearly 1200 captured. A desperate call was made for U.S. Navy air support but President Kennedy refused to give that order. Worse the anticipated popular uprising did not occur.

The blame was immediately accepted by the president but it ultimately fell on the CIA. Colonel Hawkins broke his silence on the matter year's later saying that Operation Zapata was doomed by presidential indecisiveness and lack of commitment. There is no doubt that the Bay of Pigs was a disaster from every angle, and all of the fears about exposure of U.S. involvement were borne out with negative reactions throughout Latin America and Europe. USSR Chairman Khrushchev immediately blamed the U.S. and promised support to Castro. This forced President Kennedy to reply even as the battle raged that Soviet intervention would not be tolerated. That said, the fiasco significantly weakened the new president in the eyes of the world, and no doubt emboldened the leadership of the Soviet Union.

Castro had gained a lot of political capital with Khrushchev by thwarting the invasion, and his lobbying efforts for more economic and military assistance soon paid off. Khrushchev saw President Kennedy as weak and their summit meeting in June did nothing to change his view. He welcomed the opportunity to exploit the communist foothold Castro had made in Cuba while intensifying his

Cold War initiatives in Europe by threatening to move against Berlin.

By May 1961 the Soviet buildup of Castro's armed forces had begun in earnest, focusing initially on ground weaponry. More significantly, it included three squadrons of MiG-17 aircraft and a network of ground control intercept radars that would form an air defense grid along the Soviet air force model. This buildup would continue unchecked until April 1962 when Khrushchev made a decision that would lead to a major confrontation of nuclear powers.

Meanwhile the international furor over Cuba served to encourage the Marines in VMCJ-2 to press on with their quasi-official electronic reconnaissance missions. Retired Chief Warrant Officer-4 Marty Lachow relates that despite intensive efforts by the ECMOs, signal intercepts during the initial year of VMCJ-2's F3D-2Q missions around the coast of Cuba were sparse and mainly consisted of airport surveillance and shipboard radars. The main reason, as is now known, was that the Soviets did not begin supplying Castro with numbers of military radars until mid-1961. The VMCJ-2 ECMOs became convinced the Cubans were being tipped off about their missions and were able to restrict their tell-tale radar emissions while the F3D-2Qs were flying off their coast. So, they first initiated strict radio procedures for their missions including use of lights by the control towers to signal takeoff clearance. More significantly, the squadron was somehow later on able to get permission to use friendly island nation airfields as departure bases, most notably Montego Bay, Jamaica and Nassau in the Bahamas. This allowed some unpredictable variation in the mission profiles which increased the opportunities for ELINT intercepts as well as contributing to the "Lore of the Corps" as the aircrews in civilian clothes made their way around town.

One of the most significant intercepts in 1961 was a Token multi-beam ground control intercept radar of Russian design by Sergeant Sam Figueroa. His discovery was challenged by the Atlantic Command ELINT center until he was flown to Norfolk with his tape recording to prove it. The presence of an operational ground control intercept radar at about time Cuban pilots returned home after receiving MIG-17 jet training in Czechoslovakia, gave forewarning that the Cuban air force was being significantly upgraded with modern Soviet jets and supporting command and control radars. By taking the early initiative and perseverance, VMCJ-2 was able to slowly but surely build an Electronic Order of Battle as the Soviet- supplied radars were brought on line.

In the aftermath of the Bay of Pigs fiasco, the staff of the U.S. Atlantic Command at Norfolk, Virginia developed the first of a series of related Operational Plans (OPLANs) for the employment of U.S. forces to invade Cuba and dispose of Castro's regime. Later in 1961, a covert action group was formed under the direction of Attorney General

Robert Kennedy to focus on the Cuba problem. The code word for this group was Operation Mongoose and eventually an Army general was assigned to coordinate DOD support. Joint reconnaissance centers (JRC) were established by the JCS and CINCLANT in 1962 to oversee the planning and execution of the PARPRO which involved all DOD reconnaissance and surveillance assets. Colonel Ben Skinner, then a major, was reassigned from VMCJ-2 as a plank owner in the CINCLANT JRC. VMCJ-2's F3D-2Q electronic reconnaissance missions were soon brought under CINCLANT control. A declassified DOD report to the Mongoose oversight group in April 1962 indicated the squadron was being tasked to fly 12 missions per month under the code name Call Money.

Cuban 57mm AAA Site with Whiff Fire Control Radar in 1962

CHAPTER FIVE

Missiles Discovered and the Crisis Begins

In April 1962, Chairman Khrushchev made the most serious miscalculation by a world leader since Hitler decided to invade Russia, and that was to covertly establish offensive ballistic missile systems with nuclear warheads in Cuba. A known risk taker, he planned to present his American adversaries with a fait-accompli by having his nuclear missiles capable of reaching across the continental United States operational before they were discovered. As history relates he came close to achieving his goal.

As a precursor for installation of their SS-4 medium range (MRBM) and SS-5 intermediate range ballistic missile (IRBM) systems, the Russian military knew they must first establish an imposing air defense network to include the SA-2 SAM that would likely restrict the use of the U-2 by the U.S. That would buy time for the installation of the nuclear missiles, and the SAMs would serve to defend the missiles and preclude a preemptive strike by the U.S. That meant beefing up Castro's AAA and deploying their front line SA-2 SAMs outside of their European satellites for the first time as well as MiG-21 interceptors. The Soviet Presidium authorized shipping 180 SA-2

Guideline missiles and missile units to support a network of 24 SAM sites and 48 MiG-21s, with both to be manned by Russians as there was no time for training the Cubans.

In June 1962, prior to the beginning of this massive buildup, the national intelligence agencies estimated there were only about 25 operational military radars in Cuba, all of the types reported by VMCJ-2. The estimate included about a dozen Tokens and Knife Rest early warning radars, with only six Fire Can AAA fire control radars. U-2 missions during July revealed what were likely the first SAM sites under construction without visible equipment.

After a massive sealift effort in July, the first SA-2 SAMs arrived and site construction accelerated. In mid-August, a Whiff AAA fire control radar was reported. Surprisingly, a CIA U-2 mission on August 29 showed eight SA-2 SAM sites in the western area of the island, some with radars and missiles in place. What was not known was that the SAMs and later a frontline MiG-21 squadron based at Santa Clara, near mid-island, was to be manned by experienced Russian military as well as the key nodes of the command and control network!

During this timeframe Chief Warrant Officer Marty Lachow and Staff Sergeant William "Woody" Wood, flying in F3D-2Qs on different tracks from opposite sides of the island, intercepted what appeared to be a Fan Song target tracking radar emanating from one of the newly constructed SA-2 SAM sites. The Fan Song intercept was confirmed in post flight analysis by Master Sergeant Bob Mayer and immediately reported. The National Security Agency ordered increased electronic surveillance by national assets and the first Spoon Rest target acquisition radar associated with the SA-2 was intercepted near Havana on September 15.

Shortly thereafter, Gunner Lachow recalls accompanying Lieutenant Colonel Walt Domina, the squadron commander, to a meeting of technical experts at the Navy's Bureau of Aeronautics in Washington where he was asked to describe the Fan Song intercepts. There would be more surprises to come as U.S. intelligence was lacking in many respects.

Unbeknownst to U.S. intelligence, even as the photos of the SAM sites were being analyzed, the first of the ships bringing in the Soviet SS-4 MRBMs was nearing Cuban ports and thousands of Russian "technicians" were ready to set them up and defend them! Although unaware of the plans for the nuclear missiles, the CIA and U.S. Navy had tracked and recorded an unparalleled number of ships unquestionably bringing in military cargoes to Cuba over the summer of 1962.

The need for more frequent U-2 high altitude reconnaissance missions was evident and a decision was made to transfer them from the CIA to SAC to better deal with the fallout should one be lost.

The vulnerability of the U-2 to the Russian SA-2 SAM made that possibility real. The potential need for low level photos was first surfaced in a request from the acting director of the CIA to the JCS on August 27. A heads up was passed along to CINCLANT shortly afterwards, but at a meeting of the Mongoose group on the 30th of August before the SAM site photos were available, it was decided to defer tasking of tactical assets until specific targets were identified. John McCone, the CIA director, immediately suspected the employment of the frontline SA-2s was related to protection of some high value asset like medium range ballistic missiles (MRBM), but his suspicions were not shared by the President and his national security staff. Another U-2 mission a few days later revealed more SAM sites under construction. A sobering reminder of the SA-2 threat was brought home with the loss of a CIA U-2 over China on September 9 that was flown by the Taiwanese.

On September 14, Colonel Steakley (USAF), the director of the JCS JRC, briefed the Mongoose group on the capabilities of the RF-8A and RF-101 tactical reconnaissance aircraft. Again, no decision to employ them came as the group again wanted to wait for specific targets to come from U-2 missions.

At that point a serious and never fully explained gap in photo reconnaissance coverage occurred. The number of U-2 missions authorized over Cuba was limited to two at that time due to State department concerns about losses. These missions were delayed, first to train USAF pilots on the CIA U-2s, then due to adverse weather which was a factor. But, weather delays were based on predictions not actual conditions, and partial coverage was not deemed the answer given the limited number of authorized overflights. As a result of this catch 22 it would be another month before a U-2 mission was flown over the western provinces where suspicious activity was being reported! That delay gave the Russians a full month to complete their air defense network and move forward unobserved with construction of the ballistic missile sites.

With the increasingly ominous signs of a Soviet escalation in military capability in Cuba beyond what they had provided their European satellite countries, the U.S. military was quietly preparing for execution of a CINCLANT OPLAN to invade Cuba. The JCS had no confidence in Operation Mongoose and had been pushing for a game-ending invasion for months. They confidently felt it could be accomplished without risk of a general war with the Soviet Union and with commitment of only a single infantry division. Ironically, the Marine Corps was the only service opposing this plan, believing it wildly underestimated the forces and time required to seize and pacify the large island nation. The Marines would be proven right but not for reasons they could know at the time.

Anticipating the impending need for tactical photo reconnaissance aircraft, the CINCLANT JRC developed a special plan for their employment under Operation Blue Moon. This came as the DOD implemented a new naming convention for its aircraft, with the F8U-1P's becoming RF-8As, and the USAF Voodoos' RF-101s. Under the Blue Moon plan, the RF-101s located at Shaw AFB in South Carolina under the 363rd Tactical Reconnaissance Wing, would deploy to MacDill AFB in Tampa, Florida.

Colonel Skinner recalls there was considerable discussion over the employment of the Navy/Marine Corps RF-8As, but early on the decision was made for operational reasons for them to be based at Key West and supported by Fleet Air Jacksonville's photo lab at NAS Jacksonville.

The Navy's Light Photographic Squadron 62 (VFP-62), home-based at nearby NAS Cecil Field, had 29 RF-8As assigned but less than 10 were available as most of their aircraft were deployed on Atlantic fleet carriers. The Blue Moon operation required eight full up aircraft per day which was a problem for the squadron. VMCJ-2's RF-8As were available but it was anticipated that they would be directed to provide at least a two aircraft detachment to Guantanamo with others tasked to support air strikes by the Second Marine Aircraft Wing under the CINCLANT OPLAN. One of the deciding factors was that VFP-62 had recently been training with a new forward firing KA-45 five inch format camera which also had image motion compensation needed for vertical imaging during the envisioned low level, high speed missions over Cuba. To alleviate the aircraft shortfall, VFP-62 requested a loan of four RF-8As from VMCJ-2. Major General Mangrum, the Commanding General of the Second Marine Aircraft Wing, with the support of the Commanding General Fleet Marine Force Atlantic, advised the aircraft would be forthcoming but would be flown by Marine pilots!

On October 6, CINCLANT increased its readiness posture for action against Cuba and directed secret movements of key forces to bases in the Caribbean. On the 8th CINCLANT requested JCS authorize relocation of Navy (VFP-62) and Air Force (363rd TRW) photo reconnaissance aircraft to South Florida under Operation Blue Moon. During the preceding days, the commanding officer of VFP-62, Commander William Ecker, was briefed by the CINCLANT JRC on the Blue Moon contingency plan.

On October 10, then Captain Richard Conway, the VMCJ-2 photo officer, flew to NAS Cecil in Jacksonville to attend a planning meeting with VFP-62, returning on the 11th. At the meeting, Captain Conway briefed the status of the VMCJ-2 aircraft and camera systems, noting they were equipped with older 70 MM or 2.5 inch square systems and did not have any of the desired new KA-45 forward firing cameras for installation in station one. It turns out VFP-62 only had three or four of the new cameras as well and an emergency supply order was issued to support the Blue

Moon operation. Four KA-45s from Chicago Aerial Industries were redirected to VMCJ-2 along with a team of technical representatives to install them.

Later, Lieutenant Colonel Conway recalls when the new cameras arrived the contractor technicians assisted by his Marines worked day and night to install the new cameras in RF-8A aircraft bureau numbers 144618,145611,145612, and 145635. He flew bureau number 144618 on a test flight on the 15th to check out the new cameras. This would prove to be timely to say the least as a SAC U-2 mission flown by USAF Major Richard Heyser the day before had brought back photos from Cuba that would shock the U.S. intelligence community and the world. The dark rumors coming from CIA operatives about large missiles being off-loaded at Cuban ports were confirmed. There were SS-4 MRBM sites under construction in western Cuba near San Cristobal with their launchers and missiles nearby!

President Kennedy and his national security advisors were shown the photos and briefed on the threat shortly before noon on October 16. A day later photos from another U-2 mission flown by USAF Major Rudolph Anderson Jr., showed a cluster of missile sites in central Cuba, an SS-4 site near Calabazar de Sagua, and a SS-5 IRBM site at nearby Remedios, that would threaten all major U.S. cities!

With that grim news the President and his executive committee (EXCOM) of the National Security Council went into near continuous session assessing the intelligence data that was flowing in and debating courses of action. The JCS, with USAF Chief of Staff General Curtis LeMay as the main spokesman, was clamoring for an immediate decisive air strike before the missile sites became operational, followed by an invasion with the Marines leading an amphibious assault. The President held them off hoping he had enough time to review all options and attempt to communicate with Chairman Khrushchev before risking a nuclear war by a preemptive attack. He nonetheless agreed for the JCS to increase the military readiness posture to Defense Condition Three (DEFCON 3), and authorized the largest emergency mobilization of U.S. forces since World War II to prepare for an invasion of Cuba. It seemed like everyone and everything military was headed to Florida in a matter of days. Gone was the old invasion plan, replaced by OPLAN 316, detailing an all-out, multi-pronged invasion involving over 120,000 Army armor and airborne troops and the Second Marine Division (reinforced). No more landing in a swamp at night, the Marines would come ashore east of Havana at Tarará right in Castro's face. The invasion would be preceded by sustained air strikes over several days to take out the nuclear missiles and their protecting SAMs. And of course, just in case, the Strategic Air Command was standing by to finish the job and obliterate the whole island with a string of atomic bombs.

CINCLANT executed the Blue Moon operations order on October 17 and on the 19th VFP-62 sent all of their operational RF-8As to Key West. The four plane VMCJ-2 augmentation detachment led by Captain Edgar J. Love, the squadron operations officer, flew into NAS Cecil on the 21st to have their camera systems checked out before joining VFP-62 in Key West on the 22nd. In addition to Love, the detachment included Captains Fred Carolan, Richard Conway, John Hudson and Dale Tinsley, the backup pilot. They were joined at Key West on Monday the 22th by the remainder of the squadron led by Lieutenant Colonel Domina, and the parent air group, MAG-14, commanded by Colonel Jack Conger, a legendary WW II fighter pilot and double ace. MCAS Cherry Pt. was left as a ghost town.

At 7 PM that Monday night President Kennedy went on television to inform the nation and the world that the Russians were positioning offensive missiles with nuclear capability in Cuba and he was imposing a naval quarantine to circumvent their action. He drew the line with Khrushchev by further stating *"It shall be the policy of this nation to regard any nuclear missile launched from Cuba against any nation in the Western Hemisphere as an attack by the Soviet Union on the United States, requiring a full retaliatory response upon the Soviet Union."*

As the president began his speech SAC had gone to DEFCON-3 and began dispersing its 187 B-47 bombers armed with nuclear weapons to airfields all across the U.S., including several civilian ones like Boston's Logan International. Everyone in VMCJ-2, like all of the MAG-14 units and others just arriving at Key West, knew for sure this was no drill. VFP-62 had completed planning for the initial Blue Moon missions and was on a four hour standby for the launch order expected the following morning via a newly installed hotline to the CINCLANT JRC.

In Moscow, Khrushchev had already ordered his top advisors to spend the night in their offices. Just 100 miles away Castro and the Soviet commander, General of the Army Issa Pliyev, listened to the speech and then brought their respective forces to a wartime footing. Castro dictated a headline for the morning papers declaring "Motherland or Death! We Will Win, advising the people *they shouldn't worry about the Yankees as they're the ones who should be worried about us.*" The general told his unit commanders to return to their regiments immediately to repel a possible American paratroop drop. He commanded over 40,000 Soviet combatants on the island compared to the CIA's estimate of 6-8 thousand advisors!

That night according to Dobbs, the Marine regiment selected to make the initial landing over Tarara beach was cruising off the north coast of Cuba in amphibious ships after having their pre-invasion practice exercise canceled to prepare for the real thing. He quotes a Marine sergeant leading chants by his troops exercising on the ship deck. "Where are we gonna go?" "Gonna go to Cuba." "Whatta we gonna do?" "Gonna castrate Castro!"

Meanwhile, the Marine officers involved in planning the amphibious landing were working on the details of the intricate operation much like their predecessors at Iwo Jima or Inchon. Little thought had been given to the possibility that their enemy had tactical nuclear weapons and was prepared to use them to wipe out the invasion force.

Fidel Castro and some of his revolutionaries enter Havana 1959

Cuban SA-2 Guideline Missile Site
Marine Corps History Division photo

The Soviet designed SA-2 SAM was designed to counter high altitude targets and had already shot down high flying U-2 aircraft. The complex above was in the typical star shaped pattern with the six Guideline missile launchers out at the points of the star and the Fan Song target tracking and missile guidance radar in the middle. A network of SAM sites was constructed in the July-September 1962 timeframe to protect the medium and intermediate range ballistic missiles being delivered.

VMCJ-2 ECMOs intercepted a Fan Song radar being tested before it became operational. The missile sites were manned by highly trained Soviet personnel throughout the Cuban Missile Crisis.

Medium and Intermediate Range Ballistic Missile Threat Rings

Soviet SS-5 Intermediate Range Ballistic Missile

VMCJ-2 RF-8A Over Quantanamo 1962
Photo from Hal Austin via Peter Mersky

VMCJ-2 Detachment Quantanamo October 1962
Hal Austin via Peter Mersky

Chairman Khruschev & President Kennedy Vienna 1961

CHAPTER SIX

Blue Moon Low Level Reconnaissance

As expected the launch order for the first Blue Moon missions came on Tuesday morning, October 23rd as the president badly needed close -up pictures to show the world the threatening Soviet missiles. At about noon Commander Ecker led the first of three sections of Navy-piloted RF-8As south from Key West over the Florida straits to Cuba on Blue Moon mission number 8003. He flew over a SAM site west of Havana and then on to the San Cristobal SS-4 MRBM Site No. 1 where he got a glimpse of the equipment and men working on it during his 10 seconds over the target. Another section made for airfields and SAM sites around Havana and the third to a second SS-4 MRBM site near Calabazar de Sagua in central Cuba.

As planned, the flights headed for NAS Jacksonville after completing their runs. Commander Ecker's section was the last to land after encountering a large thunderstorm nearly blocking their path back across the straits. They landed mid-afternoon where the film was downloaded and processed by the fleet photo lab. After an initial readout by Navy photo interpreters to verify coverage, the film was quickly moved on to Washington by a Navy F-8 Crusader, where the photos underwent detailed analysis at the National Photographic Interpretation Center (NPIC). Commander Ecker then flew on to Washington landing at Andrews AFB. He was met by Colonel Steakley, the chief of the JCS JRC, and escorted to the Pentagon where he was debriefed that night by the JCS still in his flight suit.

The President was presented his requested upfront and personal photos early Wednesday morning and they soon were being shown to friendly governments around the world. The photos delivered more bad news as they clearly showed the MRBM sites with launching erectors in place, missiles stored nearby and a nuclear weapon bunker under construction. All of the RF-8A's cameras came into play but the most useful was the new KA-45 that proved itself by providing incredibly detailed view of men and equipment that needed little professional interpretation.

Equally important was the tactics used matched the camera technology as related by retired Lieutenant General Hudson years later. He remembered a typical mission for a section of RF-8As, led sometimes by Navy and sometimes Marine pilots, was to photograph three or four targets. He said sometimes there were repeats, but the crews would plot different ingress and egress routes and vary their approaches to them from day to day. Taking off in radio silence using lights from the tower to taxi, they flew time/heading over the water to their ingress points at

50 feet or so then just above the treetops to proceed to their first target. With the wingman in loose trail they approached their targets at nearly 500 nautical miles an hour, then popped up to 1000 feet and turned all their cameras on to get as many exposures as possible. As soon as they passed their targets usually in about 10 seconds they again dropped back down to tree top level proceeding to their next target. After reaching their egress point they called "feet wet" and hit afterburner climbing to about 35,000 feet enroute back to NAS Jacksonville. Their assigned fighter escorts waiting off-shore from a Navy or Marine F-8 squadron would join and stay with them until they reached the mainland. Once their film was downloaded the pilots would make the short hop over to VFP-62's home maintenance base at NAS Cecil where they would remain overnight. They usually flew back down to Key West the following day.

All of the targets were selected in Washington and passed down to the squadron each night for detailed mission planning. Although the pilots did not like it they were required to make radio calls at key points along their routes once over the beach.

The Marines flew their own aircraft with VMCJ-2's Charlie Yankee (CY) tail codes and adorned with a flop-eared bunny logo. The squadron had recently adopted the Playboy call sign but had not yet received permission from the Playboy organization to use its trademark bunny logo.

Major maintenance was performed by the squadron at Key West with the Navy handling the turns at Jacksonville and most of the camera installation and maintenance. Lieutenant Colonel Conway recalls only one Marine sortie lost to maintenance and on that occasion a major hydraulics leak caused the backup pilot, Captain Tinsley, to abort his scheduled mission.

The midnight bunny painters from VMCJ-2 were very active upon arrival at Key West. Then Lance Corporal Jack Hayden Jr. and another Marine embarrassed a USAF F-104 interceptor squadron by breaching their flight line security to stencil red bunnies on their airplanes. Caught in the act, they were collared by the USAF air police and turned in to Warrant Officer Joe Stone, the squadron duty officer. Trying to keep a straight face, Stone assured the air police that they would be dealt with appropriately for such a despicable act! Before being pardoned for getting caught on the USAF flight line, they painted flop-eared bunnies onVFP-62's RF-8As, and Commander Ecker, with a sense of humor, allowed them to stay on. After an RF-8A returned from a Blue Moon mission his sailors painted a "dead chicken" alongside a figure of Castro on the fuselage as a reminder of his entourage being caught cooking chickens in their hotel room in New York when Castro visited the UN in 1960. A "smile you are on candid camera" notation also was painted on the front of many of the aircraft.

In addition to augmenting VFP-62 for Operation Blue Moon, VMCJ-2 also sent a two aircraft detachment with photo and maintenance personnel to NAS Leeward Pt. to support the defense of the Guantanamo Bay naval base. Captain (later colonel), Gerry Hintz led the RF-8A detachment along with Captain Harold Austin. They soon began flying daily missions around the periphery of the huge base in bureau numbers 145646 and 146863. The RF-8A's oblique cameras provided an extended "over the fence" view of adjacent Cuban controlled areas. At that point all dependents of Navy and Marine Corps personnel had been evacuated and the base defense reinforced by Marine ground units and a Marine Air Group.

Meanwhile upon arrival at Key West, the squadron's electronic warfare section was busy planning ECM support for the air strikes that seemed sure to come. Their main concern was how to jam the SA-2's Fan Song target tracking radar as the Marines were confident they could handle Castro's Whiff and Fire Can radars that controlled his large caliber AAA guns. All knew the SA-2 had been proven against high altitude reconnaissance aircraft but had no intelligence about its performance against tactical strike aircraft that typically delivered their ordnance from dive bombing maneuvers starting around 7,000 feet. This was in contrast to the high speed low level runs being flown by the RF-8As. The squadron EW officer, Chief Warrant Officer Marty Lachow had an occasion to brief General LeMay and his staff on their ECM plans during his visit to Key West. He did not draw a response from the crusty old SAC general who had little time for tactical aviators even from his own service. Lachow was complimented afterwards by a senior officer on LeMay's staff.

It was well known within CINCLANT that the only dedicated radar jamming assets available to support the impending operations against the sophisticated Soviet air defense systems rested with VMCJ-2's newly designated EF-10Bs and a few Navy carrier-based AD-5Q Skyraiders. At that point VMCJ-3 was alerted to be ready to augment VMCJ-2 with aircraft and aircrews.

The USAF's primary tactical ECM aircraft was the RB-66B, a modified bomber configured with a full package of barrage jammers. Since it lacked a receiving system, they were employed with an RB-66C to manage jammer employment. The RB-66Bs were all committed in Europe, although a few RB-66Cs were deployed later in the crisis period.

The squadron had arrived with its full inventory of aircraft and EW jamming systems and the ground support technicians were working around the clock to ensure they were fully operational. Upon arrival, the VMCJ-2 also began flying electronic reconnaissance missions to attempt to locate active SAM and radar controlled AAA sites, although by direction of the Soviet commander these systems were not turned on until October 27.

There were no Navy Blue Moon missions on October 24 as attention shifted to the quarantine operation and the expected "eyeball to eyeball" confrontation at sea loomed as efforts intensified to locate inbound ships with more missiles and warheads. In fact, as discovered by Michael Dobbs in research for his book, this widely advertised event never happened as unbeknownst to President Kennedy and the EXCOM, Khrushchev had already blinked and ordered several missile laden ships to return to Soviet waters. This did not change the perilous situation in Cuba much as the proverbial barn door was closed after the horse had escaped. The missiles already in Cuba were being readied for firing and it was correctly assumed some nuclear warheads were there as well. SAC was moving to declaring DEFCON-2 for the first time ever and had one eighth of the B-52s airborne 24 hours a day. The JCS was again urging the President to conduct air strikes before it was too late. Continuing low level photo reconnaissance was needed and ordered to track the progress of the missile installation and their operational status.

The Marine pilots joined their Navy counterparts on Thursday the 25th as 10 Blue Moon sorties were flown. The pilots fanned out across Cuba to cover the known missile sites and search for others. Navy Lieutenant Gerald Coffee (later a Vietnam POW) flying in the trail position of a section covering the unfinished SS-5 IRBM site at Remedios saw a large military camp off to the left of his track and instinctively decided to jink over it, take some photos, and roll back behind his leader. He had found the 146th Soviet motorized rifle regiment, (one of 3) which was equipped with the most destructive weaponry available in the Soviet army, most notably nuclear-tipped FROG/Luna tactical missiles that would deliver a 2-kiloton weapon twenty miles! He later received a letter of commendation from the Commandant of the Marine Corps, General Shoup, praising him for his alertness and bringing back *"the most important and timely information for amphibious forces that has ever been acquired in the history of this famous Navy-Marine Corps fighting team."* The planned invasion force would have not only faced first line Russian troops instead of Castro's ragtags but also would have been decimated by an unexpected nuclear inferno.

With the photos in hand from the Navy/Marine Corps team providing irrefutable evidence of the Soviet offensive missiles in Cuba, the EXCOM decided it was time to confront them head on in the only venue available, the UN Security Council. An emergency session was called and at 5 PM on Thursday, October 25th, Ambassador Adlai Stevenson, with the tell-tale photos on an easel behind him, orchestrated a dramatic exchange with his Soviet rival. Stevenson challenged him to answer yes or no to his question *"Do you Ambassador Zorin, deny that the USSR has placed, and is placing medium and intermediate range missiles and sites in Cuba,"* reminded him he was in the court of world opinion, and then told him he was *"prepared to wait for my answer until hell freezes over."* No answer was expected or necessary.

On the first two days of the Blue Moon operation, the U.S. reconnaissance aircraft had not been engaged by either Russian or Cuban air defenses on orders from Moscow. Castro was furious as it was one thing for a U-2 to fly over at 70,000 feet but the continuing low level flights by the RF-8A "hooligans" was unnerving everyone. Castro's anguish was shared by the many of the Russians as well including MiG-21 pilots at their Santa Clara base who expressed frustration about the overflights and complained they were stuck on the ground like sitting ducks.

On Friday morning October 26, the USAF RF-101s finally got in the action and returned with photos of a Soviet SAM site at Banes on the eastern end of the island that also showed radar controlled AAA manned by Cubans. Although the SAM site and supporting AAA was clearly operational, there was no attempt to fire at the RF-101s and no associated radar emissions were reported by VMCJ-2's EF-10Bs or SAC ELINT aircraft monitoring from off-shore.

Finally that afternoon Castro had enough, and believing an American air strike was imminent berated the senior Soviet commander for inaction, convincing him to at least turn on the radars that night so they would not be blind to an attack. He then ordered his air defenses to fire at the Americans and urged the Soviets to do so too. That night, a message was sent to Moscow advising that the Soviet air defense units would respond to an air attack, and the SAM batteries were placed on six minute alert to fire. That night for the first time the entire air defense radar network was up and operating including the Spoon Rest target acquisition radars supporting the SA-2 SAMs. This ominous escalation would have deadly consequences.

NPIC's David Parker pointing to Blue Moon photos of missile sites for Ambassador Stevenson and the UN Security Council on October 25, 1962
(National Security Archives at George Washington University)

Commander Ecker's photo of San Cristobal MRBM Site No. 1 from the initial Blue Moon mission on October 23, 1962

From October 23 until November 15, VFP-62 and VMCJ-2 augmentation pilots would fly seventy seven low level Blue Moon missions over Cuba to track the operational status of the nuclear missile sites. Over 160,000 negatives were brought back by the RF-8A pilots. All 12 Navy pilots and four Marine pilots were awarded Distinguished Flying Crosses for their vital contributions to U.S. intelligence during the Cuban Missile Crisis. Both squadrons would receive Navy Unit Commendations, the first ever awarded in peacetime.

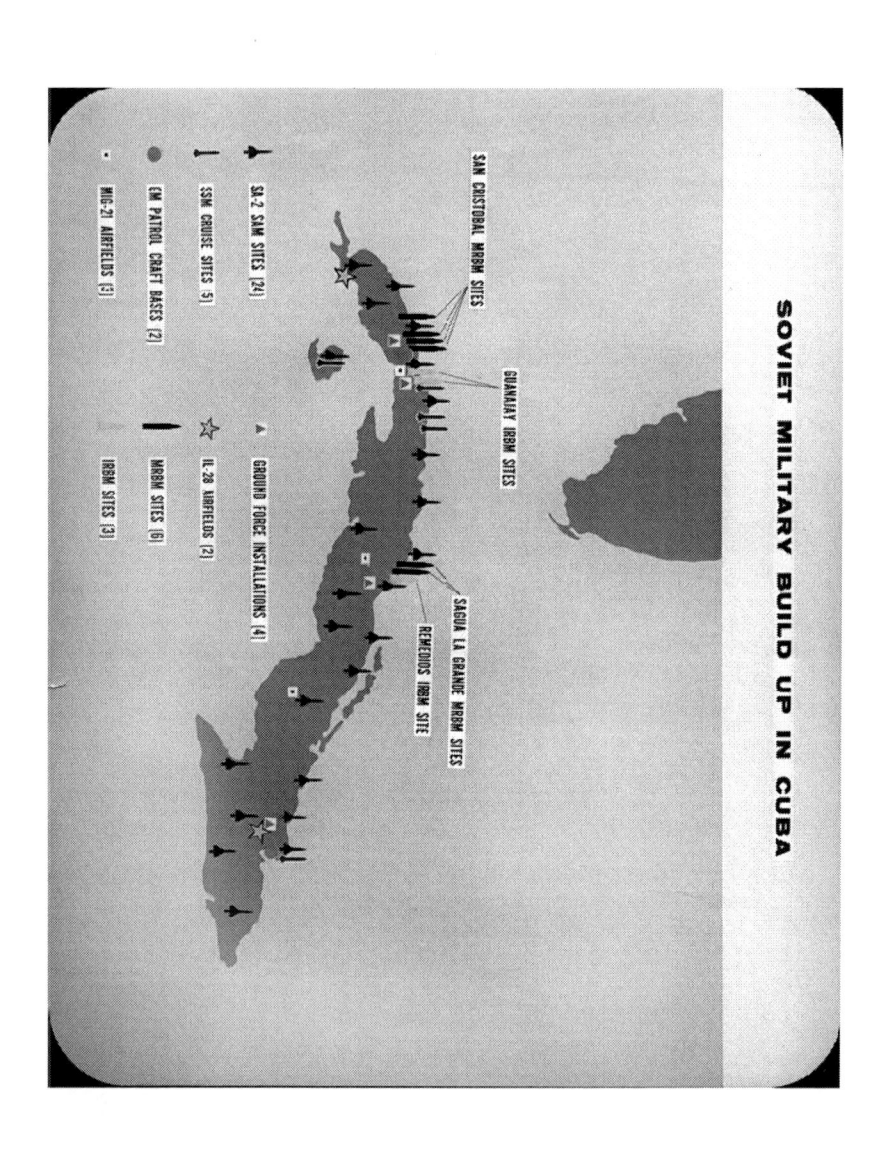

CHAPTER SEVEN

The Crisis Peaks and
Ends in Compromise

October 27th came to be known as Black Saturday due to the series of events dramatically detailed by Dobbs that seemed destined to push both the U.S. and Soviet Union into a nuclear exchange. It started early in the morning as Castro woke up the Soviet ambassador at 2 AM to persuade him to advise Khrushchev that a strike or invasion was imminent and that he saw the use of nuclear weapons as a necessary response and the Cuban people were ready to deal with the consequences. Around 3:30 AM a Soviet bomber dropped a 260 kiloton bomb on a test range near the Arctic Circle, and a few minutes later a U-2 took off from Eielson AFB in Alaska on an eight hour mission to the polar region to collect the resulting radiation fallout. The USSR had recently begun testing of nuclear weapons again and the U.S. responded in kind. Inexplicably the Cuban missile crisis caused no delays on either side.

Later that morning another U-2 aircraft piloted by USAF Major Rudolph Anderson took off from Orlando and shortly before 10:30AM was picked up on Russian radar as it crossed into Cuba heading towards Camaguey in the eastern part of the island. At the Soviet command center outside of Havana two senior generals watched as it was tracked crossing over to the southeast coast and making a turn towards Santiago and then the Guantanamo area before turning north towards the SAM site at Banes. They felt compelled to act and without contacting their commanding general ordered the Banes SAM site to shoot the U-2 down. Ironically, one of the RF-8A Crusaders unknowingly passed over the command center at the time that fateful decision was made. Their urgency was knowing that Major Anderson's photos were going to expose the Soviet plan to take out Guantanamo and its Marine reinforcements with FKR-1 cruise missiles carrying 14 kiloton nuclear payloads. The cruise missiles with their warheads had been moved to their firing position only 15 miles from the base the night before!

Fed by inputs from his Spoon Rest target acquisition radar, Lieutenant Colonel Ivan Gerhenov, the Banes SAM site commander, switched on his Fan Song target tracking radar, acquired the U-2, and shortly thereafter fired two missiles bringing it down when a proximity fuse from one detonated close to the aircraft. Off shore, a SAC RB-47 and the USS Oxford SIGINT ship had intercepted the SAM radars but were unaware of the U-2 mission and had no means to warn Major Anderson anyway. It was 11:19 AM in Washington but the Pentagon and the president would not know for sure that the U-2 was shot down and Major Anderson's body recovered until around 6 PM. Meanwhile, a SAC B-52 dropped an 800 kiloton bomb at the Pacific test site on Johnston Island at 11:35 AM as scheduled. Minutes later at 11:46 AM, the U-2 on the radiation sampling mission was lost, and 1000 miles off course, entered the Soviet Union over the Chukot Peninsula penetrating hostile airspace for 300 miles before turning back. When advised of this later President Kennedy shrugged it off saying "There is always some SOB who doesn't get the word".

The Kremlin and Khrushchev would first learn about the unauthorized shoot down of the U-2 from the Pentagon's 6 PM announcement. It raised serious concerns about communications with their commanders in Cuba, or worse a break down in discipline. In retrospect, it appears this event, alarming as it was to both the Americans and the Soviet leaders, was the final straw in both drawing back from the brink.

On this fateful day, the Navy-Marine Corps Blue Moon team would fly 14 sorties, the most since the operation began. Nearly all of the pilots would report being fired upon by Cuban AAA and several would bring back photos to prove it. All the missile sites were revisited as part of a frantic search for the nuclear warheads and updates on their launch status. The airfields were also targeted to locate suspected IL-28 bombers capable of delivering nuclear bombs. Captain, (later colonel) Love took off in bureau number 144618 at 3:41 PM as part of the six sorties scheduled for that afternoon. He led a section that was assigned to cover the SS-4 and SS-5 sites in central Cuba, then the major Russian MiG-21 base at Santa Clara.

Colonel Love recalls coasting in over the beach resort of Varadero and flying southeast for about eight minutes until he picked up the Calabazar de Sagua SS-4 missile site near some low humpbacked hills above the fields of sugar cane. He took some oblique shots of the site and then headed for Santa Clara. As they passed the airfield he saw a flight of MiG-21s (40 based there) about to land and banked steeply to his left to avoid them. Luckily they either didn't see him or chose to ignore him. He turned back to the north towards the SS-5 IRBM site at Remedios and as the pilots popped up to take their photos he saw a puff of smoke from AAA fire from his right. He broke sharply away from the fire and nearly collided with his Navy wingman who had come in too close. Both switched on their afterburners and soon were safely out over the water heading to Jacksonville. What he could not know was the nuclear warheads for the SS-4 MRBMs at Calabazar had arrived just two hours before and were temporarily stored in vans about a mile from the missiles. His photos would show this site was fully operational, and with its nuclear warheads available was capable of destroying New York City some 1290 miles away that night! Another Blue Moon mission that afternoon discovered IL-28 bombers being put together at San Julian airfield on the western tip of Cuba, but these were to support the Cuban Navy unlike the ones still in their crates at the eastern airfield at Holquin, who had already had their Tatyana 12 kiloton nuclear bombs available.

The EXCOM met that afternoon and on into the evening trying to make sense of the attacks on the American aircraft and conflicting letters from Khrushchev. They knew the U-2 was missing but did not know how or why, but the word from the returning Blue Moon aircrews was quite clear about them receiving AAA fire. At that time, the Navy had intercepted and was trying to force a Soviet Foxtrot class submarine to surface but did not know it had torpedoes with nuclear warheads on board, and the captain authorized to use them in self-defense. When they received confirmation that the U-2 was shot down by a Soviet SAM, the discussion quickly turned to what if anything to do in retaliation. The military had planned to conduct strikes against any SAM site that fired on unarmed aircraft but the JCS now considered any attack should be against all of the SAMs. All soon saw that option may result in launching of the nuclear missiles. The JCS had set in motion plans to commence military action the following Monday. Time was of the essence to try for a final deal with Khrushchev.

At about 8:30 PM Attorney General Robert Kennedy met with the Soviet ambassador telling him time was running out and outlined the president's offer to not invade Cuba if the missiles were immediately pulled out. He verbally gave him a commitment that was not going to be put in writing and that was for the U.S. to quietly remove its Jupiter missiles from Turkey in a few months. His meeting was followed by a formal message to Moscow with a deadline for an answer by 9 AM in Washington the following morning. Khrushchev, knowing this was the time to back away, cabled his commander in Cuba to immediately stand down and start dismantling the missiles. Later, in a Radio Moscow broadcast intended for President Kennedy, he stated the USSR had decided to dismantle Soviet missiles in Cuba and return them to the Soviet Union. It was received about 9 AM in Washington on Sunday morning October 28, 13 long days since the missile sites were first discovered on film.

The JCS was understandably skeptical fearing another Soviet deception. It was not to be, but tactical reconnaissance was again urgently needed, this time to verify the dismantling of the missiles and track their movement out of Cuba. Captain Love flew one of the four Blue Moon sorties on Monday the 29th that allayed a lot of fears as indeed there was clear evidence the sites were being dismantled. The Marine pilots continued to support the Blue Moon operation as missions were scheduled nearly every day until November 15 tracking the retrograde movement.

On November 5, Captain Carolan was flying as wingman for Lieutenant Commander Tad Riley monitoring the movement of missiles out to a port in central Cuba when he spotted a pair of Russian MiG-21s making a run on them. The pilots hit their afterburners and turned sharply into the MiGs before hitting the deck and heading out over the north coast at Mach 1.2. The MiG flight leader gave chase for 20-30 miles but gave up as he couldn't gain on the Crusaders. Riley later related that Carolan had no trouble keeping him in sight as he was leaving a rooster tail of dust every time he went over a plowed field. They later learned the Russians were on a training mission and they too were unarmed but anxious to do something to harass the American pilots that regularly flew over their airbase.

On November 10th in celebration of the 187th birthday of the Marine Corps, an all- Marine section led by Captain Hudson with Captain Carolan on his wing flew a Blue Moon mission monitoring the missile removal.

Operation Blue Moon missions were suspended on November 16 and the Marine commitment was over on November 17. All five pilots would return to Key West on November 26 to participate in a VFP-62 formation as President Kennedy presented the Marine augmented squadron a well-deserved Navy Unit Commendation. One of the Navy RF-8As with its red bunny clearly showing served as a backdrop in pictures of this historic formation. Commander Ecker, along with 11 of his pilots and the four Marines were awarded Distinguished Flying Crosses for Operation Blue Moon. The Marines and most of the Navy pilots received their medals from Admiral Robert

Dennison, CINCLANT at a later ceremony in Jacksonville. Months later at MCAS Cherry Point, VMCJ-2 would receive the Navy Unit Commendation for its extended exceptional service from September 1, 1960 until December 1, 1962. This would close out the most important chapter in the squadron's illustrious history.

Commander Ecker (l) shaking hands with Captain Hudson

This photo was taken at Homestead AFB after the two pilots flew in for a USAF sponsored press conference after the conclusion of Operation Blue Moon. Note the "dead chickens" on the RF-8A in the background.

**VMCJ-2 and VFP-62 pilots received DFCs for
Operation Blue Moon from Admiral Dennison,
CINCLANT in a ceremony at NAS Cecil Field.
Captains Conway and Carolan are standing
with Hudson and Love kneeling in front.**

All four pilots would go on to complete their careers in
the Marine Corps. All but Hudson would serve multiple
tours with the Marine Composite Reconnaissance squadrons.

THE SECRETARY OF THE NAVY
WASHINGTON

The Secretary of the Navy takes pleasure in commending

MARINE COMPOSITE RECONNAISSANCE SQUADRON TWO

for service as set forth in the following

CITATION:

"For exceptionally meritorious service during the period 1 September 1960 to 1 December 1962, in connection with the planning and executing of aerial reconnaissance missions in support of operations of the utmost importance to the security of the United States. The consistent and outstandingly high record of accomplishment attained by Marine Composite Reconnaissance Squadron TWO attests to the professional competence, diligence, and resourcefulness of its officers and men. Their inspiring and zealous devotion to duty in the face of adverse circumstances reflects great credit upon themselves and the United States Naval Service."

All personnel attached to and serving with Marine Composite Reconnaissance Squadron TWO during the above period, or any part thereof, are hereby authorized to wear the NAVY UNIT COMMENDATION Ribbon.

Paul H. Nitze
Secretary of the Navy

CHAPTER EIGHT

Smoke Rings after the Crisis

Once the missile crisis was over the Marines resumed their pattern of monthly electronic reconnaissance missions around the periphery of Cuba for training as well as ELINT collection. Tactical reconnaissance over the island was forbidden, but VMCJ-2 continued to provide periodic photo coverage of Guantanamo. The RF-8As were replaced by RF-4Bs Phantoms in 1965. Although the offensive nuclear weapons were gone and most of the Soviet troops had departed the island, Castro's substantial military forces remained, and in fact his air defenses were much more capable than they were before the crisis began. Although no one expected any immediate trouble out of Castro, the United States intelligence community was determined not to again be surprised by what the unpredictable island dictator might do.

Periodically, U-2 high altitude reconnaissance missions over Cuba were authorized, and since the Russians had left Castro with about 30 SA-2 SAM launchers and trained operators, an attack authorized by the egotistical dictator could not be ruled out. In any case, the reaction of the Cuban air defense network to the overflights was always of interest to the intelligence agencies. The U-2 flights were often used as ELINT collection opportunities, and the Marine EF-10Bs were scheduled to fly their electronic reconnaissance missions to coincide with them. The unclassified code word for their missions was changed to Smoke Ring in later years.

The Smoke Ring missions were scheduled on approved tracks under the PARPRO with oversight by the CINCLANT joint reconnaissance center. The JRC looked to the Joint Air Reconnaissance Control Center (JARCC) at Key West to provide radar coverage for threat warning and control of all of the missions. Strict procedures were instituted to preclude international incidents due to inadvertent violations of Cuban airspace, nominally set at 20 nautical miles off-shore. Nevertheless, over the years several unplanned events did happen.

The inherent navigational limitations of the EF-10Bs, namely no radar and reliance on line-of-sight electronic navigation aids, often put the aircrews at risk, if not from Castro's air defenses, then from the wrath of higher headquarters. One Smoke Ring track took them south out of Key West then east down the length of the island on the north side and then around to the southeast terminating at Guantanamo. Another track originated either from Guantanamo or from Montego Bay in Jamaica south of Cuba. This track would bring the Skyknights along the south coast then around the western tip and north past the Havana area before recovering at Key West. The EF-10Bs were often out of range of navigational aids and radio communications on long segments of these approved tracks. This required the aircrews to revert to use of dead reckoning navigation, and that coupled with reduced visibility due to weather conditions created many opportunities for violations of Cuban airspace. The old hands just shrugged off these incidents noting that they served to increase their intelligence take.

Retired Captain Meek Kiker, a veteran ECMO, recalls being in one of those radar "dead zones" after departing Guantanamo on a track around the eastern tip of Cuba and then up along the north side. He made a rare intercept of a Fire Can fire control radar while his pilot was supposedly flying a westerly track parallel to the northern coast which was obscured by a cloud deck. His direction finding display showed the short ranged radar signal emanating from the nose of the aircraft instead of off the left wing. Looking down he caught a glimpse of the ground below. After escaping the island they learned the air control center had been frantically trying to warn them but apparently they had lost HF radio contact. That resulted in a quick trip home and imposition of a new rule for a mandatory abort if communications were lost and the coastline was not visible.

Unpredictable weather often was encountered during these long missions and kept the pilots busy as they were responsible for navigation and fuel management while the

ECMOs concentrated on ELINT collection. The most interesting, and surely the most retold story of a weather related incident, involved a pair of EF-10Bs on an extended range mission out of Montego Bay back to Key West in November, 1963. Then Captain Richard "Cat" Conway , one of the famed Blue Moon RF-8A pilots, was leading the flight when they encountered unexpected very strong winds that was forcing them off course. He soon realized that they did not have enough fuel to make it back to Key West or return to a U.S. air field. They were near the Yucatan peninsula and Conway smartly decided to divert to a Mexican air force base near Cozumel. After a safe landing they were warmly greeted by their surprised hosts and after some delay the JRC was informed. They returned to Key West the following day without further incident. What they did not know according to Colonel Skinner, who was still at the CINCLANT JRC, was that about the same time as their divert, a U-2 had been lost off the coast of Florida due to unknown circumstances after completing its mission over Cuba. Needless to say the two incidents created a lot of urgent message traffic to and from the Pentagon. To add to the irony, President Kennedy was assassinated just a day later and suspicions of Castro being involved quickly arose.

In late 1965, VMCJ-2 received the first of their new Grumman EA-6A Electric Intruders and about four months later deployed them to Key West to fly Smoke

Ring training missions. The EA-6A, still in development at the time of the missile crisis, was the first purpose-built tactical electronic warfare aircraft and superior in all respects to the venerable EF-10Bs. It would quickly prove its worth during the on-going Vietnam War. But it was the same Marine EF-10Bs that were at the ready to support air strikes against SAMs in Cuba in 1962 that were first called on to counter the identical sophisticated Soviet air defense systems in Vietnam in 1965.

With the introduction of the EA-6A Electric Intruder, VMCJ-2 became responsible for training all replacement aircrews for VMCJ-1 which remained engaged in combat in Vietnam until 1973. To that end, the Smoke Ring missions provided an excellent opportunity for the ECMOs in training to experience a realistic threat environment before deploying to Vietnam. On occasion, the Marines were reminded that Castro's air force still posed a threat. On at least three missions during the 1970s, the EA-6As were intercepted by Cuban MiG-21 Fishbeds. The author was involved in the first of these encounters in 1970 which came close to turning into a dogfight between our Marine fighter escorts and Castro's MiGs. The complete story is related in the epilogue.

In 1975 VMCJ-2 was decommissioned and transitioned into Marine Tactical Electronic Warfare Squadron-2 (VMAQ-2), dropping the photo reconnaissance mission. VMAQ-2 would continue the deployments to Key West and the Cuba PARPRO missions as part of its EW training program, first with the EA-6A Electric Intruders, and then the EA-6B Prowlers in the 1980s. By this time SAC's SR-71 Blackbird had taken over the periodic high altitude reconnaissance missions over Cuba from the U-2s.

The Castro regime escalated its support of international communism in Africa (Angola) as well in Central America in the late 70s and early 80s with continuing help from the Soviet Union. Several events in late 1981 and early 1982 resulted in President Ronald Reagan signing out two top secret national security directives dealing with Cuba. The first was signed on January 4, 1982 and dealt with Cuban support of communist movements in Nicaragua and El Salvador. Cuba was added to the State Department's list of countries sponsoring international terrorism. On January 14th a Soviet ship configured to neutralize efforts to detect nuclear submarines reached a Cuban port. The next day a National Security Council meeting was convened to deal with this new provocation which was viewed as violating the 1962 security pact regards offensive capabilities. On January 19, another directive was issued in response to the Cubans receiving a large quantity of new swing-wing jet aircraft believed to be the ground attack variant of the Soviet MiG-23 Flogger. Under presidential orders, increased surveillance of Cuba was ordered along with a heightened state of readiness of U.S. military forces in Florida and the

Caribbean area. There were other actions taken to increase the visibility of the U.S. military in the region.

After an ill-advised ban on overflights by President Carter ended in late 1979, the SR-71 missions were resumed. During this timeframe the Cubans began to turn their SA-2 missile guidance radars on without launching in an attempt to disrupt the SR-71 missions.

With President Reagan's directive, a series of SR-71 missions was scheduled commencing in January 1982. In conjunction with these missions, then Major Don Pardue recalls VMAQ-2 receiving urgent national tasking to deploy an EA-6B Prowler detachment to Key West to conduct electronic reconnaissance operations. Then Lieutenant Colonel J.D. Weber, the VMAQ-2 commander, led the first contingency deployment. The squadron followed this initial deployment in January with two plane EA-6B detachments for several months running.

VMAQ-4, a reserve EA-6A squadron, was stood up at NAS Whidbey Island in 1981 and made periodic training deployments to Key West through the 1980s as well. Then Captain D.R. Lawler and Major Marshall Smith assigned to the active duty support group (MAG-42 Detachment Charlie), recalled an incident in May 1985 that showed Castro's intelligence network was feeding his air defense radars with data on the Electric Intruder flights. Normally, two EA-6As flew together on their pre-approved tracks and for the most part Castro's air defense radars did not oblige them by radiating during their time on station. One day to change things up the two aircraft split up the section after arriving at their normal initial point about 50 miles south of Key West. One aircraft flew the normal track to the west then reversing near Havana and flying east down the long side of the island. The other EA-6A turned in the opposite direction and flew on to the eastern tip before reversing and joining back up with the lead to return to Key West. The VMAQ-4 commanding officer, Kari Johnson, led this mission which coincided with an SR-71 overflight. The split track provided better coverage of the entire island during the short time the SR-71 was over land and resulted in a spike in radar activity. Later after debriefs, it seems from radio intercepts that the Cuban air controllers were tipped off that the Electric Intruders were coming but were initially confused by their unorthodox tactics.

The last of the Electric Intruder missions around Cuba was early in 1989 as VMAQ-4 transitioned to the EA-6B Prowlers after the Persian Gulf War began. This was same year that the Soviet Union crumbled and Castro's guardian angel was no more.

Ironically, Marine Corps aerial reconnaissance operations against Cuba began with Fidel Castro in power and 50 years later he remained the leader of the longest tenured communist government in the Western Hemisphere. When he finally stepped down from power in favor of his brother Raul in 2008, he had been a thorn in the side of 11 U.S. presidents.

An early VMCJ-2 EA-6A Electric Intruder and EF-10B Skyknight in 1965

Note the official Playboy bunny had replaced the original flop-eared bunny on the squadron logo by 1965.

VMAQ-2 EA-6B & EA-6A over N.C. Outer Banks
February 17, 1977

Bureau number 160432 was first USMC Prowler and bureau number 147865 was the oldest Electric Intruder. The EA-6As went to the Navy reserves during the transition to the Prowlers. VMAQ-4, a Marine reserve EA-6A squadron, stood up in late 1981 and periodically deployed to Key West for training. The last PARPRO missions were flown by VMAQ-4's EA-6As in January 1989. VMAQ-2 continued to deploy to Key West for training and flew PARPRO missions around Cuba throughout the 1980s as well.

Epilogue

Castro's Revenge?

(Previously published in *Foundation*, Volume 30, Number 1, Pensacola, Spring 2009)

Marine Composite Reconnaissance Squadron Two (VMCJ-2) based at MCAS Cherry Pt. N.C. was the Eyes and Ears of the 2nd Marine Aircraft Wing from 1955 until 1975 flying photo reconnaissance and electronic warfare aircraft. In addition to its operational mission it was also responsible for replacement aircrew training for VMCJ-1 which was permanently deployed to WESTPAC in 1960. Castro's Cuba became VMCJ-2's sandbox back in 1960 shortly after his revolutionary government began receiving military aid from the Soviet Union. For 15 years Cuba would be the geographic backdrop for execution of both of the squadron's missions. VMCJ-2 was the first Marine Corps unit to receive the Navy Unit Commendation in peacetime for aerial reconnaissance operations over and around Cuba from 1 September 1960 until 1 December 1962, culminating with the Cuba Missile Crisis. During the famous 13 days of October and beyond, VMCJ-2 provided four RF-8A Crusaders and pilots to augment VFP-62 for the crucial low level photo missions that tracked the Soviet nuclear armed ballistic missiles as they became operational and then their subsequent dismantling and removal under the Kennedy-Khrushchev pact. In addition, the squadron's EF-10Bs kept tabs on the air defense radars from Key West, and another RF-8A detachment was deployed to Guantanamo Bay to support base defense efforts much as they had during the two previous years of the massive Soviet military buildup in Cuba.

I well remember those uncertain days of October 1962 as I was then a senior at the University of Florida awaiting graduation the following spring and commissioning as a 2nd Lieutenant. With that doomsday averted, I entered active duty and after attending the officers Basic School went on to Pensacola for nugget training as one of the Marine Corps' first Naval Flight Officers. After basic NFO school, I was selected for further training as an ECMO, supposedly to be one of the first to fly the new EA-6A Electric Intruder. In 1964 when the program slipped, I found myself checking out in the venerable EF-10B Skyknight in VMCJ-3 at MCAS El Toro.

Then a thing called the Vietnam War happened and we deployed to Danang in October 1965 to become VMCJ-1. After 13 months supporting TF-77 and 7th AF operations over North Vietnam I caught a break with a set of orders to Hawaii to become a plank owner in the CINCPAC Joint Reconnaissance Center, a three year tour. My time there was most interesting to say the least as not only did we have our hands full with operations over Vietnam, but during my watch the USS Pueblo was captured and a VQ-1 EC-121 was shot down by the North Koreans. I mention this as background for a little known incident during my follow-on assignment to VMCJ-2.

I was a captain when I joined VMCJ-2 in January 1970 for transition training in the EA-6A prior to going back to WESTPAC. Later that Spring I was joined by Lieutenant Colonel Chuck Houseman, a veteran VMCJ pilot who was enroute back to Vietnam before becoming the CO of VMCJ-1 in Japan in 1971. By the end of April, we both had accumulated a good bit of time in the aircraft and as one of our last training events we were assigned to lead a section of EA-6As down to Key West for a couple of days to fly ELINT training missions around the periphery of Cuba. These missions, dubbed Smoke Rings, had long become routine as VMCJ-2 had been flying them to keep track of Castro's air defense radars and provide ECMO training since 1960. This one turned out to be far from routine!

Our skipper, Lieutenant Colonel Jimmy Green, was fortunate to have a sharp and rather aggressive squadron air intelligence officer as his S-2 who was on top of the military situation in Cuba. He had been monitoring the increased message traffic regarding Cuba taking part in OKEAN-70, the Soviet Navy's first ever global exercise involving over 200 ships. A Soviet task force had been operating out of a Cuban port and a series of TU-95 Bear flights to and from Cuba from the Kola Peninsula had been reported. Although the Soviet pilots had left Cuba in 1963 after turning over their MiG-21s to the Cubans, Castro's fighter pilots were by 1970 reasonably well trained. They had also gotten more aggressive as just a few days before our mission some of his MiGs had intercepted a civilian light plane that had wandered into Cuban air space. We learned later that there was some background chatter about Castro itching to flex his muscles with some kind of air Pueblo-like incident.

The day before we were scheduled to depart for Key West, the S-2 approached the CO with his concerns that the Cubans might consider our flights during the OKEAN exercise as provocative and cause some kind of trouble. He also reminded him of a provision in the CINCLANT order covering our "training missions" for fighter escorts to be assigned at the discretion of the CG 2nd MAW, something that had never been done before.

The next morning they briefed the CG, his G-2, and other key staff. The CG at that time was Major General Marion Carl who was not one to back off from a challenge and quickly okayed tasking MAG-31 at MCAS Beaufort to provide us fighter escorts. Aside from his heroics as an ace fighter pilot in WW II, General Carl allegedly flew some rather interesting photo missions in Banshees over the coast of mainland China right after Korea while he was CO of VMJ-1.

To MAG-31 the tasking had to be both good news and bad news. In 1970 after 5 years in Vietnam concentrating on CAS missions our F-4 community had about lost its base of experience in air-to-air intercepts, and full mission capable aircraft were a rarity. However, just the thought of having a remote chance to engage a Cuban MiG put the fighter jocks into a frenzy and they quickly adopted VMCJ-2's "Can Do Easy" motto!

VMFA-451's Warlords were tasked to support us and received the word to get four aircraft with missiles at the ready down to Key West ASAP. The squadron had just transitioned from F4Bs to F4Js and beset with the attendant training and maintenance problems had to scramble to cobble together four up aircraft and weapon systems.

Meanwhile, Chuck and I arrived in Key West as a single ship around noon as our wingman went hard down in the chocks at Cherry Point. The VMFA-451 aircraft didn't make it until later that evening, and Chuck recalls some of the flight crews only had tennis shoes as they didn't have time to go home after being recalled from a squadron party.

Needless to say our Marine gaggle arriving unannounced caused a lot of consternation with the tenant activities. We were summoned to report to the CO of the Joint Air Reconnaissance Control Center (JARCC), an Air Force colonel, who was really ticked off about the Marines bringing in fighter escorts. He had not been briefed on the possibility of a Cuban reaction to our missions, and just saw us as complicating his life. Finding we were acting with written authority, he instructed us all to show up early the next morning for a briefing by his controllers on exactly how they would require our missions to be conducted so we didn't screw up as he put it.

Upon arrival the VMFA-451 aircrews were grilled by their hosts, VF-101, the resident Navy F-4J RAG. VF-101 had been maintaining a 24/7 strip alert for some time and didn't buy the need for our CAP. I guess their questioning led to a rather heated exchange with the Marines who wondered which side they were on. When order was restored, the Navy CO advised the Marines that he was confident they could handle anything the Cubans put up, but if they were hell bent on flying a CAP the next day he'd loan them some good missiles and get his avionics section to help get their systems up and ready.

We were tasked to fly missions in the morning and afternoon on our pre-approved tracks at 25,000 feet that required us to come no closer than 20 nautical miles to the Cuban coast. Our track would first take us down the length of the island on the north side where we would reverse course and fly back to a turn point off Havana, then onto our southwest leg down to the western tip, reversing back to the turn point off Havana where we would head back to Key West some 90 miles away. Due to fuel limitations the Marine F-4s were to split into two sections and directed to operate from orbits assigned by the JARCC instead of following us in trail. As briefed, we were assigned a different controller and radio frequency from the fighters, but the JARCC plan was for the fighters to be switched over to our frequency in the event of any trouble.

The morning mission went down more or less as planned with no reaction by the Cuban air force. I recall detecting a couple of fire control radars along with the usual early warning and GCI radars we expected to see. In the afternoon again everything seemed okay as we approached the last turn point off Havana to turn for home. The early warning and GCI radars were again very active throughout the mission so there was no doubt we were being tracked by the Cubans. As we came abreast Havana it was bright and clear and at our altitude I could almost pick out the San Antonio de los Banos MiG base southeast of the city.

Within minutes after turning north for Key West we got a call from our JARCC controller advising we had "strangers" at six o'clock at 10 miles!! Needless to say this rang our bells and we began calling for more info and got it with a higher pitched voice telling us that the so called strangers were now at 5 miles and closing! Chuck had already picked up our speed and started a weave so we could get a better look behind us. At this call he chopped the throttles and went for the deck in a serious defensive maneuver and then firewalled the engines as we ran for home low over the water. We got a glimpse of our adversaries flashing by over us, Chuck recalls there were 3 but I only saw two delta wing MiG-21s. All this time we were screaming at the controller who had gone silent asking where our CAP was as the F-4s should have been immediately switched over to our frequency. Minutes later we were back within sight of Key West where we landed forthwith, never hearing from the fighters!!

Chuck climbed out of the aircraft and commandeered a vehicle to take him straight to the JARCC where he found a rather shook up colonel who had lost his "I am in control here" attitude and was hard pressed to explain what had gone wrong. Turns out his senior controller had been on the golf course leaving our "routine" mission to junior controllers. I joined up with the VMFA-451 crews who were equally upset and we all gathered in a rather chaotic JARCC conference room with everyone yelling at each other it seemed. I found myself gesturing with my hands like some kind of top gun, but at same time asking about the range of a MiG-21's Atoll missiles.

From the debrief we found that our F-4s had just made their section turnover with their drop tanks still on when their controller gave them a vector and told them to go to burner without saying why. They soon were going too fast to jettison their tanks and found they were being vectored in on a flight of MiG-21s who by that time were racing back to Cuba, flying straight and level. The F-4 lead rolled in on the tail end Charlie and got a Sidewinder growl while asking for instructions, never having heard any of our frantic radio calls. At this point, as we were clear the JARCC was not about to give them the order to fire and they broke off and headed back only to then find out that we had been intercepted. The JARCC track on the MiGs showed them well inside our ADIZ after overshooting us and turning back south.

We were told later that the MiGs had been cleared to fire but never found out for sure. In any event Castro got a little revenge on one of the squadrons that exposed his missiles to the world and Chuck and I have the dubious distinction of being intercepted by his MiGs inside our own Air Defense Identification Zone!

Needless to say there were high level phone calls and message traffic going all the way up and back to Washington with more questions than good answers forthcoming. The upshot was we returned to Cherry Pt. that night and the squadron didn't fly any more Cuba missions for a while. They never again had fighter escorts.

Unbeknownst to us we picked a bad day to be involved in an international incident, or then again maybe not as things quieted down fast. Turns out the Pentagon and President Nixon that very day had announced our incursion into Cambodia and the press was all over him.

On the following Monday (May 4th) the Time magazine cover story was about the Soviet government by committee which had just celebrated the anniversary of Lenin's rise to power, and the increasingly menacing

Soviet military activity in the Western hemisphere. In fact they were already planning to build a nuclear submarine base at Cienfugueos which later in the year nearly caused a repeat of the 1962 missile crisis. Of note, just two weeks after our incident Castro sent a flight of MiG-21s over the Bahamas to intimate the island government who was detaining some Cuban fishermen.

There were at least two more intercepts of Marine EA-6As in the 70s. The first involved the squadron CO then Lieutenant Colonel (later Major General) Royal Moore Jr. The last was in 1977 and the aircrews took the picture below to record that "friendly" incident in international airspace.

VMAQ-2 EA-6A BuNo 156988 trailed by a Cuban MiG-21 in 1977 (photo by Pete McGrew)

USAF SR-71 BLACKBIRD

USAF U-2